THE JOY

OF

CHINESE COOKING

Additional titles in the
HIPPOCRENE INTERNATIONAL COOKBOOK CLASSICS

All Along the Danube
by Marina Polvay

The Art of Israeli Cooking
by Chef Aldo Nahoum

The Art of Syrian Cookery
by Helen Corey

THE JOY

OF

CHINESE COOKING

Written and Illustrated by

DOREEN YEN HUNG FENG

HIPPOCRENE BOOKS, INC.
New York

Originally published by Grosset & Dunlap, New York.
Hippocrene Books, Inc., paperback edition, 1992.

For information, address:
Hippocrene Books, Inc.
171 Madison Avenue
New York, NY 10016

ISBN 0-7818-0097-8

Printed in the United States of America.

Contents

INTRODUCTION   11

I. China in Your Kitchen   13

     How to Cook the Chinese Way   13

     Ingredients Used in the Making of Chinese Dishes   20

     Utensils Used in the Making of Chinese Dishes   37

     How to Plan a Chinese Meal   41

     Chinese Dinners and Table Utensils   44

     Equivalent Weights and Measures   54

     Cantonese Pronunciations   55

II. Appetizers   56

III. Chinese Soups   74

IV. Egg Dishes   87

V. Fish and Shellfish   94

VI. Poultry   110

VII. Pure Meat Dishes   130

VIII. Vegetable Dishes   145

IX. Rice and Mien Dishes   160

7

CONTENTS

X. Chinese Desserts   169

XI. Chinese Tea   179

XII. Chinese Festival Dishes   182

     New Year   182

     The Lantern Festival   186

     Festival of the Flowers   189

     Ching Ming   191

     The Dragon Boat Festival   197

     The Herd Boy and the Weaver Maid   202

     All Souls' Day   207

     Festival of the Moon   211

     The Kite Flying Festival   215

     Festival of the Winter Solstice   218

INDEX OF RECIPES   221

8

List of Illustrations

Straight slicing and diagonal slicing 15

Adequate methodical preparation 17

Ingredients cooking in a *wock* 19

Pea sprouts and bean sprouts 22

Chinese scallion and Chinese parsley 23

Haw laahn dow, Chinese pea 24

Geung, fresh ginger root 25

Lien ngow, lotus stem 25

Fooh gwaah, bitter melon 26

Wun yee, cloud ears 27

Doong gwooh, Chinese mushrooms 28

Hoong joe, Chinese red dates 28

Gum jum, golden needles 29

Lien jee, lotus seeds 29

Baak haap, One Hundred Unities 29

Tiem jook and *fooh jook* 30

Jook sün, bamboo shoots 30

Maah tuy, water chestnut 31

Baat gok, Chinese star anise 34

Ngung faah yuk, five-flowered pork 36

Beef plate and navel 36

Chinese *wock* 37

Homemade steamer 38

Cleaver 38

Chopping-block 39

Chinese pastry board and rollers 40

Light cooking utensils 41

Arrangement of *wuy deep* on table 47

9

LIST OF ILLUSTRATIONS

Chinese table seating	48
Serving dishes	49
Table utensils	50
How to hold chopsticks	51
Turnover with scroll edging	58–59
Bonnet-shaped pouch	62
Wun tun dough being folded in layers	67
How to fold *chün gün* No. 2	72
Chinese watercress	77
How to prepare winter melon pond	83
Pictograms of Sheung Period	95
Chinese method of gift-wrapping paper-wrapped chicken	114
How to prepare a blown duck for roasting	128
Methods of hunting and trapping (Yin Period pictographs)	130
Ceremonial plowing	131
Yin Period pictograph representing the word "male"	146
The sacred lotus	148
Yin period pictographs representing plowing, year, and harvest	161
The Eight Treasures	169–172
New Year	182
God of the Kitchen	183
The Lantern Festival	186
Faah Seen, Goddess of the Flowers	190
Comforts rising to the spirit world in the form of smoke	192
Race of the dragon boats	196
How to wrap *Joong*	199–200
Herd Boy and Weaver Maid	203
Loong ngaan, dragon's eyes	204
How to prepare a watermelon basket	205
Dey Jong Wong, gentle God of Hades	208
Sheung Aw seeking refuge in the moon	212
The Kite Flying Festival	214
The Three Plenties	217

Introduction

FOOD, besides being an absolute necessity for existence, is one of the few pleasures which span the entirety of the human lifetime. For this reason, the joy of eating is given great importance in China; and cooking, through the decades, has been dreamed and fussed over, in times of want as well as in times of plenty, until it has ceased to be plain cooking, but has grown and developed into an art. Food has been represented through other mediums of art, especially poetry, literature, and folklore; and these tales and food beliefs have been handed down, from generation to generation, with ever-increasing glamor. Every aspect of food is analyzed, from its palatableness to its texture, from its value to its effectiveness, and from its fragrance to its colorfulness; until, as in other works of art, proportion and balance are instilled in every dish.

To possess the services of a good Chinese chef in one's home is like having a prima donna in close vicinity. He includes all the talents of a connoisseur with the knowledge of an herb doctor, the sensitiveness of a mother-in-law, and the benevolence of a clucking hen. He once held the title of *Daai See Mo* 大 司 務 which means "Grand Charge of Cuisine Affairs," and through the ages his title has grown in dignity and expanded to *Daai See Fooh* 大 司 傅 which identifies him as the "Grand Maestro of the Culinary Arts." Being a *Daai See Fooh*, he must be handled with the diplomacy and gentleness learned through time and experience. No *Daai See Fooh* will remain in your home unless he loves you; and lucky and to be envied are those blessed with his solicitous attentions over the satisfaction of stomach and health through the delicacies of his works of art and the science of *leung-hay* and *yeet-hay*.

11

All foods in China, besides possessing an ever-evolving tale and history, are divided into two large categories: those which have the property of heating the human system and those which induce cooling effects. The literal translation is that all foods exude either *leung-hay* 凉 氣 "cool air," or *yeet-hay* 熱 氣 "hot air"; but I shall not attempt to use these literal translations again, because I was once stopped in the midst of my attempt at elucidation by the retort of one gentle critic who said, "How very, very complicated —and to think that the only musical foods I have ever known are beans and cabbage!"

People abroad with enthusiasm for Chinese food are largely divided into two types: those who are exuberant over CHOP SUEY (to such an extent that in wartime Chungking they inspired huge placards with the tempting legend "Genuine San Francisco Chop Suey Found Here") and those super-gourmets who wax poetic in their exotic discourses on such mysteries of the palate as shark's fin, birds' nest soup, and ancient eggs. Chop suey is known to us Chinese only as an agreeable foreign dish, and as for shark's fin and birds' nest soup, lucky are the few who have had the opportunity to taste such delicacies.

What prompts me to write this book is the desire to introduce to people abroad the joys of preparing and indulging in the tastiness of Chinese dishes enjoyed by a large number of our 475,000,000 people. There is no mystery involved in Chinese cooking, unless knowing what ingredients to use and where to purchase them and how to substitute for those which may be unobtainable can be called mysteries. All this is merely necessary information, which this book will, I hope, painlessly reveal and so bring joy, excitement, and a little bit of China into your kitchen, home, and life.

Chapter I

CHINA IN YOUR KITCHEN

HOW TO COOK THE CHINESE WAY

THE cooking of most Chinese dishes requires a maximum of preparation and a minimum of fuel and cooking time. Through the centuries, Chinese cooking has adapted itself to an ever-present shortage of fuel. The most frequently used methods of cooking are:

1) *CHOW* 炒 (a) *frying:* a small amount of oil is heated in a frying pan before the ingredients are tossed in to be constantly stirred and mixed until the foods is done; (b) *braising:* the ingredients are fried only until blended and well coated with hot liquid grease sufficient to keep them from burning when covered by a lid to cook a while in their own juice or in very little liquid until done or almost done.

2) *MUN* 炆 *fricasseeing:* the ingredients are first fried or braised or browned and then simmered slowly in stock, sauce, or gravy until cooked.

3) *JING* 蒸 *steaming:* the ingredients are cooked in a container suspended above water level within a larger container holding sufficient water to generate steam through boiling.

4) *HOONG SIEU* 紅燒 *red-stewing:* the ingredients are first fried or braised and then stewed slowly in a sauce which consists of a large percentage of soya sauce.

13

5) SIEU 烧 *roasting, barbecuing,* or *grilling:* meat is usually roasted in an oven or upon a spit or rack over direct heat and basted with a highly seasoned sauce.

6) JI'AAH 炸 *deep-fat frying:* enough oil to cover the ingredients is heated to such a degree that the ingredients will be fried to a rich golden brown outside and be thoroughly cooked inside.

7) DUNN 燉 *steaming and double-boiling,* at the same time: the ingredients are first fried, braised, or browned, and then set in a narrow tall pot with a generous amount of stock. This pot is placed in a larger pot and immersed in boiling water, which generates steam. Care must be taken that the outside water level does not reach beyond the halfway mark of the height of the smaller pot.

Maximum preparation of ingredients before cooking is absolutely necessary if one desires to keep peace of mind, remain unflustered, and cook a good meal. The experienced cook will have all the materials well prepared and neatly set out within easy reach; because, once the food hits the pot upon the fire, the rest usually follows with cyclonic rapidity.

Meat should be prepared, sliced, or chopped, mixed with flavorsome ingredients, and allowed to soak at least ten minutes. Vegetables should be thoroughly cleaned, peeled if the recipe calls for it, sliced, chopped, or diced, and laid aside in neat piles upon a dish. Dried ingredients should be soaked in cold water until spread out, cleaned of unwanted particles, and resoaked in fresh warm water until soft. Then they should be taken out, drained, and placed alongside other prepared vegetables. The flavored water in which the ingredients soaked the second time should be kept. This water adds tastiness if used when the recipe calls for the addition of water in the making of sauce or for dissolving cornstarch for cooking.

In the case of all fleshy and fibrous vegetable stalks, the meat and the stalks are cut perpendicularly across the grain to insure tenderness and succulence after cooking. Meats can be more easily and finely sliced if frozen slightly stiff before being used. But if meat is frozen, more time should be given for the meat to thaw out and soak in the sauce. If you cannot find time to stiffen the meat in the refrigerator before slicing, and the technique of paper thin slicing is difficult for you in the beginning, do not get upset, because this annoyance can be easily remedied. Place the slices of meat flat upon the chopping board and pound them briskly once with the flat of the cleaver. This extra treatment is in any case advisable for slices of beef before cooking.

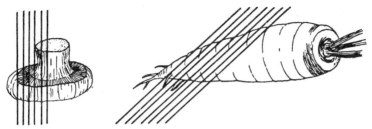

Straight slicing and diagonal slicing

Two methods of slicing are used for meats and vegetables. *Straight slicing is* used with tenderer meats and with such vegetables as scallions, parsley, or mushrooms. Coarse-grained meats and such nonperishable vegetables as carrots, celery, ginger, and some cabbages are *diagonally sliced*. This method of slicing allows for a larger area cut across the grain to be exposed to the heat in cooking, and for the absorption of flavors.

Dicing of ingredients means cutting the ingredients into cubelets in sizes varying anywhere from $1/16$ to $1/2$ inch. *Mince-dicing* is from $1/16$ to $1/8$ inch. *Fine-dicing* is from $1/8$ to $1/4$ inch. *Average dicing* is usually about $1/3$ inch.

Chopping or *mincing* is cutting up the ingredients without regard for definite shape. Chopped food is coarser than minced food. The latter resembles food that has been put through a

15

grinder. A grinder is frowned upon, however, because although the meat may be just as finely minced, it has not gone through the workout a pair of cleavers or just a single cleaver gives it. In using cleavers, try to find a drum tempo to chop to. If it is peppy enough, it will make the mincing procedure much more rhythmic and less tedious. To mince to a *pulp*, or as the Chinese say, *yoong* 融 "melt," chop with the blunt edge or the top of the cleaver blade after the meat has been minced fine with the sharp edge of the blade. If you continue to chop with the sharp edge to the bitter end, however, the result will be bitter indeed, for the board surface will begin to "melt" along with the ingredient. Not even a dog deserves to have a tinge of *jum-baahn may* 砧 板 味 "chopping-board flavor" in his food.

To facilitate the chopping or slicing of such slippery ingredients as cloves of garlic, scallions, celery stalks, or ginger slices, place the flat of the cleaver over the ingredient and pound or press the cleaver down. You decide between pounding and pressing after you have decided how slippery the ingredient is. You can smash down upon a clove of garlic or a slice of ginger, but just try it with a scallion, or better yet with some peanuts! ... After the object has been pounded or pressed, it will lie more tamely on the board and thus facilitate chopping and slicing.

I stress again the importance of maximum preparation, neatness, and systematic arrangement, for these will smooth the road toward the joy of Chinese cooking. Proceed as you do when you are going to bake a cake. In this case you would think it natural to be all prepared. The baking pan will be greased and dusted with flour, the flour will be sifted with other dry ingredients, the sugar and shortening will be creamed, the eggs set aside, the liquid measured, and the oven will be heated. And so, in the same way, be systematic and prepare all the ingredients for a Chinese dish. This will save you time, miles of walking, annoying hunting, rushing, nerves, and temper.

So, clear a large table and set out a pile of deep saucers about 6 inches in diameter, several bowls, the bottle of soya sauce, vegetable oil, salt, pepper, sugar, and a box of cornstarch. After you prepare the meat, place it in a bowl, mix it with whatever flavorsome ingredients you plan to use, and allow it to soak. Then prepare the ingredients to be fried with it and place them on top of the meat. These ingredients are usually minced garlic or ginger.

Adequate methodical preparation

Next prepare all the vegetables, fresh or dried, and place them all in neat individual stacks in one of the deep saucers. Chinese cooks always stack their vegetables neatly and separately, for they allow for that slight difference of cooking time required for different vegetables. Longer-cooking vegetables such as onions, bell peppers, and celery naturally go into the pan first. Tender vegetables such as parsley would logically go in last. If *jup*° 汁 "gravy" is

° *Jup* is the correct Cantonese word for "gravy," but since the word is phonetically the same as that meaning "to arrange dead bodies," many unused, mix the ingredients for that and set the bowl next to the dishes containing the meat and the vegetables. Next, decide on the pots, pans, and lids you will be needing and set them out. Finally, decide on the serving dishes and lay these out. Now, and only now, are you ready to start your cooking with the peace of mind and assurance which come from adequate preparation.

Although a measuring spoon is added to the list of utensils and ingredients in the illustration, I wish to mention that such a contraption is taboo in a Chinese kitchen. The *Daai See Fooh,* like the artist, measures by the sensitiveness of discerning eye and hand. An artist, however, is good only after he has trained himself to measure the quality of weight and balance of color, line, and texture in his own individual way. But this individualism, which gives so much pleasure, is based on the technical and scientific laws of esthetics.

Throughout the following pages of this book you will find measurements, sizes, textures, colors, and techniques. It is my hope that you will train yourself to observe and to measure these qualities eventually by eye, touch, smell, taste, and even by sound;° because, once you have learned these techniques, you will realize the excitement of being able to cook with dabs and pinches and indulge in your own gifts of ingenious inventiveness, which will lead to individualism and ultimately to your achievement of the rightful title of *Daai See Fooh.*

---

sophisticated people prefer not to use this spine-tingling word and substitute *"wu-suey,"* meaning "glue water," which, by the way, is phonetically the same word as that meaning "lake water."

° At one time our *Daai See Fooh* tried to teach me the technique of listening to a squab cook to a finish in deep fat. I was to listen for a certain squeal of rawness issuing from the sizzling hot oil. Before I could distinguish the sound among other cooking sounds, he declared that it had vanished and that the squab was done! The squab was all rich golden brown on the outside and cooked to a juicy tender finish on the inside.

To come back to the process of cooking, if the ingredients are to be fried, braised, or browned, always heat the pan first, and then pour in the oil and heat it until it is thin and easy-flowing before adding the ingredients. When oil or water is required during the cooking, the addition should be made by pouring the minimum of either down the side of the pot or pan. Water additions should always be hot, unless the recipe specifically calls for cold. When sauce or gravy is added, a hollow should be made in the center of

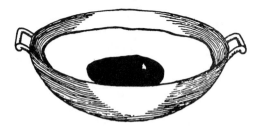

Ingredients cooking a *wock*

the ingredients, exposing the bottom of the pan, and the sauce poured into this hollow. Then when the sauce is slightly heated and cooked, it may be stirred and mixed thoroughly into the ingredients. A kettle of boiling water singing on the hearth is quite necessary in a Chinese kitchen. In the making of custards, always add warm liquids instead of cold, for this results in a creamy smoothness, whereas cold liquids will produce an uneven rubbery texture full of air holes.

All Chinese food is thoroughly cooked and yet extremely wholesome. Very little or no water at all is used in the majority of the recipes, since the Chinese Quick Cook Method brings out the natural juices from the meat and vegetables. This is sufficient and tasty; and almost nothing is more abhorrent to a Chinese than to find his dinner bogged down in a gluey sea of pseudo sauce composed chiefly of water and a thickening agent.

When cooked, meats must be exceedingly tender; and sometimes, if the recipe calls for it, the skin or surface must be *chûy* 脆 which means "crisply crackling and fragrant." When we say "exceedingly tender," we mean that all meats after cooking should possess the succulence of velvety chicken. Vegetables must retain their individual characteristics, flavor, and color. Chinese cooking preserves all this plus the quality of freshness. In some cases, as with the onion, leek, and other strong-flavored ingredients, a longer period of cooking is employed to allow the strong flavors to lose most of their identity within the blend while yet adding just enough to give a touch of teasing subtlety to the savor of the whole dish.

The food when being served must be well composed and attractive on the dish, for well-prepared food deserves that introduction which will brighten the curious eye, excite the palate, and whet the imagination and appetite. Food must also be either delicate enough to be broken into dainty pieces by chopsticks, or else already in small enough segments to be lifted to the mouth in polite morsels.

INGREDIENTS USED
IN THE MAKING OF CHINESE DISHES

THE secret of Chinese flavors is easily discovered once a person knows the basic kinds of sauces, herbs, spices, dried and pickled fruits or vegetables that are used in Chinese cooking. There are also certain cuts of meat and varieties of fresh vegetables used exclusively for Chinese dishes; but if one cannot obtain these easily, substitutes can often be used without too much difficulty or harm to the actual recipe. Cuts of meat like *ngung faah yook* 五花肉 "five-flowered pork" and *ngow baak naam* 牛百腩 "hundred abdomen of beef," not usually found in one's neighborhood butcher shop, can be wheedled out of any butcher with a soul. Vegetables such as *ngaah choy* 芽菜 "pea sprouts" and *daai dow ngaah* 大豆芽 "bean sprouts" can even be cultivated in one's own kitchen. We Chinese prefer freshly killed fowl, and since that is not our preference alone, they may be found in many a poultry shop. The Chinese also like their fish with both the head and skin on if eaten unfilleted; and the fish must be as recently killed as possible before being cooked. As a result, one usually trips over tubs of tail-flicking swimming fish scattered all over the typical unglamorized Chinese grocery shop abroad. It is a pity that many people cannot bear to look at a fish with its head on, on a platter, for they thus miss experiencing the delicate taste of fish heads. At times I can sympathize with them, for I too have known what it is to be slightly hypnotized by the stony stare of a reproachful fish eye. But this proffer of sympathy is not intended as license to skin and behead the fish unless the recipe calls for fillet.

Wherever there is more than one Chinese family in a city or town abroad, there is almost inevitably also a Chinese restaurant or grocery shop in the vicinity; so it is always possible to obtain one or more of the basic ingredients for flavoring. Of these basic ingredients, the soya sauce is absolutely essential. *Jeung yow* 醬油 "soya sauce" can nowadays be found in almost all neighborhood delicatessen or grocery shops.

In the following pages I shall explain various popular basic ingredients which go to give dishes characteristic Chinese flavors. The more illustratable objects will be fully drawn so you will be able to prowl around a Chinese grocery shop and get what you want by merely pointing. Everything is out on wild display; so it is much easier to point than to try to pronounce the Chinese names. The latter method, however, never fails to please the storekeeper and you will as a result make a very valuable friendship.

1 *Ngaah Choy* 芽菜 *Pea Sprouts.* People generally mean pea sprouts when they say bean sprouts. Pea sprouts are tiny shoots

issuing from a little pea. When bought, the pea sprouts often still carry an olive-green hood, which should be plucked off during the washing. If the roots at the tail of the snow-white stem are too long, they should also be plucked off.

Pea sprouts should be used the same day they are purchased. However, if you plan to keep them overnight, wash them thoroughly, pluck off the clinging green husks, and drain them in a large sieve which will enable the air to circulate through them. If the husks are left on, or if the sprouts are kept in a bowl, they will turn gray during cooking, acquire a musky flavor, and generate a

1. Pea sprouts 2. Bean sprouts

sour odor. The easiest way to get off most of the husks during the washing is to submerge the sprouts in a pot of cold water. As they rise to the surface, keep plunging them down a few times, and then as the husks come loose from the sprouts and submerge, skim up the floating sprouts and remove them to another container. Unless you have the patience of Job, it is practically impossible to get off all the husks. Be satisfied if you get most of them off.

It is quite easy to grow pea sprouts at home. A perforated or nonrust mesh rack can be used. Suspend this rack over a basin, cover it with a double layer of wet cheesecloth, sprinkle a layer of tiny peas over this, and cover them in turn with another layer of wet cheesecloth. At frequent intervals sprinkle water generously over the cheesecloth. See that the water drains properly, and when the basin is full, pour the water out, for once the water becomes slightly stagnant, your pea sprouts will absorb all of the musky unpleasant odor. Pea sprouts are edible and ready when they are about one inch long (5 days to one week).

2 *Dow Ngaah* 豆 芽 *Bean Sprouts.* They are usually golden yellow in color and possess a strong flavor and a rather crunchy texture. The hood color varies according to the type of bean used. This hood must be removed. Care of the bean sprout is similar to that of the pea sprout. The bean sprout, however, takes much longer to cook.

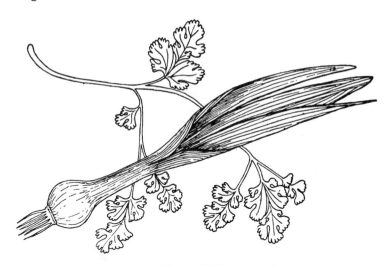

Chinese scallion and Chinese parsley

3 *Choong* 葱 *Onions.* Chinese love onions, and they grow many, many varieties. Of these the scallion is most frequently used. The white onion 大 葱 *daai choong*, the leek 大 韭 菜 *daai gow choy*, a special favorite and delicacy called simply *gow*

23

choy, and garlic both fresh and dried are used. *Gow choy* can be described as looking somewhat like a mixture of chive leaf and scallion leaf. It is very long, narrow, and flat. Some possess a bluish-green color, others the insipid color of a faded leek. Garlic cloves must be firm, full, and ivory under the pink crisp skin. Old, stale dried garlic imparts an unpleasantly heavy flavor to cooking.

4 *Yien Say* 芫荽 *Chinese Parsley.* Unlike the frilly dark-green variety one usually finds in grocery shops, Chinese parsley resembles the fragrant and tasty variety called cilantro found in Mexico. This parsley contains a willowy graceful stem, has flat, serrated leaves, and is of a clear medium green. The blue-green, frilly, bristly type is good for garnishing a dish, however, and will add color and brightness to your masterpiece.

5 *Haw-Laahn Dow* 荷蘭豆 *Chinese Pea.* There is a terrible confusion of names here. The literal translation of *haw-laahn dow* is Dutch beans, but in the United States these delicious beans are known as Chinese peas. Most continental Europeans call them French peas, and the French call the peas *mange tout.* Some Scandinavians call them sugar peas or snow peas.

Haw laahn dow, Chinese pea

6 *Baak-Choy* 白菜 *Chinese Cabbage.* The name *baak-choy* really means "white cabbage," but it is generally known abroad as Chinese cabbage. *Baak-choy* is a white longitudinal leafy vegetable about 9 to 12 inches long. The older leaves are often tinged with pale green.

7 *Geung* 薑 *Fresh Ginger Root.* A tuber with a hot spicy flavor, it resembles a scrawny potato with a lot of tiny potatoes sprouting

24

out all over it. Under that brown scaly skin, however, the pungent ginger is of a rich ivory color. The dried, ground variety should never be used as a substitute for the fresh. It is better to omit

Geung, fresh ginger root

ginger from the recipe altogether if you cannot obtain fresh roots. The older the ginger is, the sharper the spiciness and the more fibrous the tuber. If you are lucky enough to obtain very young ginger root, these tender, delicate, fiberless tubers impart a deliciously subtle flavor to anything with which they are cooked. They are also excellent if marinated in vinegar, oil, and sugar; and they are delicious candied.

Lien ngow, lotus stem

25

8 *Faahn Gwaah* 番 瓜 *Vegetable Marrow* or *Chinese Squash.* A green cucumber-looking vegetable with thin yellow stripes. *Faahn gwaah* in Chinese really means "foreign melon." When the long variety of squash cannot be obtained, the flat round variety may be used in its stead.

9 *Lien Ngow* 蓮 藕 *Lotus Stem.* The red-brown, starchy, tuberous underwater stem of the water lily plant. When the stem is cut diagonally, the hollow passages running lengthwise form a circle of holes in each slice (see page 25).

Fooh gwaah, bitter melon

10 *Fooh-Gwaah* 苦 瓜 *Balsam Pear,* commonly known as *Bitter Melon.* A clear green *leung hay* vegetable. It is about the size of a cucumber and possesses a wrinkled surface. Inside is a layer of white or pink spongy pulp and seeds. This must be removed before cooking. When cooked, bitter melon gives a cool but slightly bitter flavor, to which one may habituate oneself. The presence of quinine in the vegetable accounts for the bitter taste.

11 *Pickled Cabbage.* When you go into a Chinese grocery shop, you will usually have to pick your way between tubs of live fish and open barrels of pickling Chinese cabbage. Among these the most popular are: *haahm choy* 鹹 菜 salty cabbage, *choong choy* 冲 菜 onion pickled cabbage, and *mooi choy* 霉 菜 fermented cabbage.

To ease your curiosity as to how cabbage is pickled, I shall give the recipe for making *mooi choy*. This recipe has not been tested by myself, for I find it much simpler to go out and buy the stuff, and you will soon find out why!

Sun 10 pounds cabbage, called *ghaai choy*, for 2 days. Dissolve 1 pound salt in water and allow cabbage to lie therein with a heavy slab of stone holding it submerged and pressed. After 6 or 7 days, wash cabbage clean of all foreign particles. Dry cabbage in sun until thoroughly dehydrated, and then steam until tender. Repeat procees of sunning and steaming four times more.

12 *Chaah Gwaah* 茶 瓜 *Tea Melon*. A delicious amber-colored pickle full of peppy crunchiness. It may be eaten cold as an accompaniment to *congee* or it may be steamed with meat.

Wun Yee, cloud ears

13 *Wun Yee* 雲 耳 *Cloud Ears*. A type of cultivated fungus full of tonic quality. In its dried state it looks quite unimpressively like shattered slate shingles, but when soaked it visibly stretches itself out luxuriously until it resembles a beautifully shaped brownish gelatinous ear.

14 *Doong Gwooh* 冬 菇 *Chinese Mushrooms*. Dried, brownish, black-capped mushrooms. They range anywhere from ½ to 2 inches in diameter when dry, and they expand slightly when soaked. Another dried variety of mushroom used in China is the grass mushroom 草 菇 *cho gwooh*, tall, thin, lanky, but extremely tasty. It cannot be obtained easily abroad, but the large dried

27

Italian mushrooms make a perfect substitute. The favorite fresh mushroom used by the Chinese is the pretty little pug-nosed button mushroom 磨菇 *maw gwooh.*

Doong gwooh, Chinese mushrooms

If fresh mushrooms cannot be obtained at certain seasons, use the canned variety which come whole. Mushrooms can be dried at home cheaply and will last indefinitely. Buy the mushrooms when they are in season and cheap. String them through the center of the stem and cap about one inch apart. Hang the strings in the sun for a few days until the mushrooms are dried. Then hang them in a dry airy room and use the mushrooms whenever you wish.

Hoong joe, Chinese red dates

15 *Hoong Joe* 紅棗 *Chinese Red Dates.* Little red dates with patent-leather skins, withered to a peanut-shell quality. After they are cooked, they swell and have an enticingly sweet flavor. *Hoong joe* are often used in soups, desserts, and fish dishes.

16 *Gum Jum* 金針菜 *Golden Needles.* Dried lily flowers in

short lengths and of a burnished—gold color. They possess nutritive values and are cooked with fish, poultry, or vegetables.

Gum jum, golden needles

17 *Lien Jee* 蓮 子 *Lotus Seeds.* Delicately flavored little nuts with dark-brown husks. They are usually added to festival dishes,

Lien jee, lotus seeds

since lotus seeds are a symbol of fertility. (The name is phonetically identical with the words meaning "continuation of births of sons").

18 *Ho See* 蠔 豉 Dried *Chinese oysters* of a red-brown autumn-leaf hue. These tasty mollusks are used to impart some of their strong delicious flavor to soups, stews, and sometimes semi-vegetarian dishes.

Baak Haap, One Hundred Unities

19 *Baak Haap* 百 合 *"One Hundred Unities."* Dried pearly-

white fleshy petals of a plant related to the species lilium. As a matter of fact, there are more superstitions and traditional associations than real benefits involved in their use.

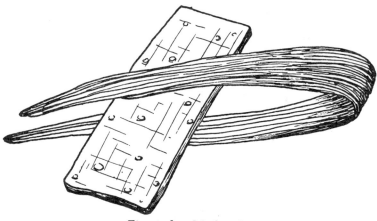

Tiem jook and *fooh jook*

20 *Tiem Jook* 甜竹 and *Fooh Jook* 腐竹 Products of the soya bean. The soya bean milk when boiled separates into various

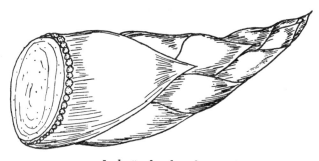

Jook sün, bamboo shoots

layers; the rich cream that rises is called *fooh jook*, and the settling sediment is called *tiem jook*. When dried, they look like stiff boards

30

glazed with enamel, but after they have been cooked they become creamy and gelatinous. *Tiem jook* is used in fish dishes; while *fooh jook* is usually cooked in soup.

21 *Jook Sün* 竹 筍 *Bamboo Shoots.* There are two varieties of canned bamboo shoots, the salted and the unsalted tender young shoots. Unless the recipe calls for the salted variety, use only the fresh shoots (see page 30).

22 *Maah Tuy* (horses' hoofs) 馬 蹄 *Water Chestnuts.* May be bought fresh, but they also come neatly cleaned and peeled in cans. In Mexico, a water plant called *jícama* can be substituted for water chestnuts and bamboo shoots. This vegetable resembles both the water chestnut and the bamboo shoot and is much more economical and easier to procure.

Maah tuy, water chestnut

23 *Bow Yü* 鮑 魚 *Abalone.* Comes dried or in cans. The canned variety is by far the easier to use since it is cured and prepared. The important thing with canned abalone is to cook it as little as possible, for the longer it is exposed to heat, the more rubbery and tough it becomes. Abalone is a mollusk with a thin elongated shell. The outer surfaces are faintly ridged and crossed by smaller, close-set ridges. The uniformly brown surface is also covered with little holes which rise into waterproof tubercles. Abalone shells are a good source of high-grade mother of pearl.

One seldom finds occasion to use up an entire can of any one

31

ingredient. The best method of keeping left-over bamboo shoots, water chestnuts, or abalone is to place them in clean pint-sized jars, cover them completely with cold water, seal them with an airtight lid, and then place the jars in the warmest part of the refrigerator. The water should be changed every two days at least.

24 *Jeung* 醬 *Chinese Sauces.* Come in bottles or cans. If brought in cans, it is best to transfer them immediately upon opening to clean, lidded jars and store them in the warmest part of the refrigerator.

a *Jeung Yow* 醬油 *Soya Sauce.* An almost black sauce made from the soya bean. The best substitute when soya cannot be obtained is Maggi.

b *Ho-Yow* 蠔油 *Oyster Sauce.* A delicious addition to many ingredients. It is a thick grayish-brown liquid, which is usually sold in bottles.

c *Fooh Yü* 腐乳 *Bean-Curd Cheese.* Grayish-white little cubes of pressed bean curd fermented in strong wine. *Fooh yü* may also be used in cooking.

d *Naam Yü* 南乳 Bean-Curd Cheese, Eastern style. Prepared in a brick-red sauce. *Naam yü* is usually used for cooking.

e *Saang See Jeung* 生豉醬 A semi-solid mass of aromatic red beans. It is one of the more popular sauces used in cooking.

f *Dow See* 豆豉 Tiny black fermented beans, which are generally crushed and added to such other strong-smelling ingredients as fish. The bean adds a delightful spiciness to the sauce.

g *Hoy Sien Jeung* 海鮮醬 Another famous red sauce which delights the palate. It is often used in cooking shellfish and ducks. Many people remember it as the delicious sauce that is served with Peking roast duck.

For the benefit of those curious souls who may want to know what goes into the preparation of bean-curd cheese, I shall give an ancient recipe:

Cut large slices of fresh bean curd into a size about 1 inch by 1 inch by ½ inch. Soak in salt water for 3 or 4 days. Then place in sun for 2 days to dry. After that, steam until extremely tender. Sun another day and then place in bottles with aromatic sauces of a clear color and generous amounts of wine of strength and quality. Cover tightly with lid and allow bottle to stand in sun for another day.

25 *Gon Yiu Chee* 江蹈柱 *Dried Scallops.* A powerful source of added flavor for congee and soups. These amber-colored disks come about ½ inch deep. The coarse deep-sea variety is extremely nutritious. Deep-sea scallops are 2 to 3 inches in length when caught. Then they are cut across the grain into ½-inch-thick disks.

26 *Chinese Spices.* Chinese cooks usually have quite a well-rounded knowledge of spices and herbs, and they often employ these aromatic gems in frugal quantities in order to enhance the flavor and fragrance of the dishes they are making. The five spices most frequently used may be purchased mixed or singly, whole or powdered. If purchased mixed, one asks for *ngung heung* 五 香 "spices of five fragrances." If purchased in powdered form, one asks for *heung new fun* 香 料 粉. If purchased separately in crude, whole form, one asks for any one of the five spices described below:

a *Baat Gok* 八 角 *the Chinese Star Anise* (Illicium anisa-tum). An evergreen shrub which grows to be about ten feet high and yields an eight-pinnacled star-shaped fruit. (*Baat gok* means "eight horns.") When dried, the fruit is of a deep burnt sienna, and each pinnacle serves as a pod holding a shiny ocre-brown seed which possesses very fragrant volatile oils which aromatize and flavor the ingredients with which they are cooked. The star anise is one of the favorite spices used in Chinese red-stewing. Medicinally it serves as an excellent stomachic and carminative.

Baat gok, Chinese star anise

b *Wooi Heung* 茴 香 *Fennel* (Foeniculum vulgare). A perennial plant two to six feet in height which produces fruits and seeds yielding highly volatile oils with aromatic tastes and odors. The shiny pale green fennel seeds are elliptical and arched in shape, about ⅜-inch long and ¼-inch wide. Like the anise, they are also valued for their carminative properties.

c *Faah Jiu* 花 椒 *the Anise-Pepper of China* (Xanthoxlum piperitum). A small thorny tree about ten feet in height with unequal pinnate leaves dotted with transparent spots which are really cysts filled with volatile oils. The small greenish-white flowers arranged in terminal clusters may be polygamous or unisexual. The fruit is a deep scarlet globose pea-like drupe with a bony kernel enclosing a single blackish-red seed. The tiny fruit possesses a pungent aromatic flavor, and is the favorite spice for cooking with strong-flavored ingredients such as fish.

d *Ding Heung* 丁 香 *the Clove Tree* (Jambosa caryophyllus). A beautiful evergreen which attains a height of forty feet. The pale green flowers grow in numerous groups of terminal clusters, and gradually achieve an intense bright red color by the time the flowers are ready for picking. The dried, deep-burnt-sienna-colored cloves possessing a powerful odor and a hot acrid taste are the unexpanded flower buds. When pressed, cloves exude a volatile oil which is both tonic and carminative.

e *Yook Gwuy* 玉 桂 *Chinese Cinnamon* (Cinnamomum cassia). A coarse type of cinnamon tree with a thick woody bark and a less delicate flavor than the true cinnamon, which has a wonderful fragrant smell and a moderately pungent taste accompanied by a slight degree of sweetness and astringency. Cinnamon, when used in medicines, is considered one of the best restorative spices and is excellent as a carminative.

27 *Mei Jing* 味 精 *Essence of Flavor.* A white powder which when added to other ingredients in small quantities does not impart a discernible flavor of its own but helps to bring out the natural flavors of the cooking. *Mei jing* is usually used for soup and pure vegetable dishes.

28 *Oils and Fats.* Vegetable oils like the soya bean oil, salad oil (Mazola or Wesson), peanut oil, and castor nut oil are excellent for Chinese cooking. Sesame seed oil is excellent and delicious, but like olive oil it is frightfully extravagant. Vegetable oils should be used in Chinese cooking because they have an extremely high smoking temperature and are not likely to burn. They also absorb practically no food odors from the cooking ingredients and thus may be used over and over again. Fats and oils with low-smoking temperature not only soak into food but also impart unpleasant odors and taste.

For making pastries and ·*deem sum* 點 心 (see page 56), Chinese always use *jüh yow* 豬 油 strained pork suet. This suet may either be obtained from pork drippings or else may be suet which has been specially purchased for the purpose, melted down, strained, cooled, and resolidified. It is not advisable to use any other shortening than *jüh yow* when making Chinese pastry. In Mexico *jüh yow* may be bought as *manteca de unto.*

29 *Meats*. Some typical cuts are:

    a *Ngung faah yook* 五花肉 *five-flowered pork*. A cut of meat which closely resembles salt pork, only it is not salted.

Ngung faah yuk, five-flowered pork

It has a layer of skin, and then four or five alternate layers of fat and lean tissue, ending with a generous layer of lean meat. Five-flowered pork is taken from the loin side of a pig.

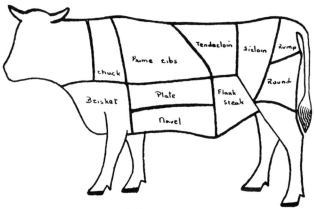

Beef plate and navel

    b *Ngow baak naam* 牛百腩 *hundred abdomen of beef*. A coarse cut of meat full of muscle and strong fibers. After

36

long, slow cooking, it becomes soft and gelatinous and is both nutritious and tasty. This cut of meat comes from an area called Beef Plate.

It is my hope that these often inadequate descriptions may be of some help, and also that through the pictures you will be able to recognize old friends when you come across the actual ingredients in a grocery shop.

UTENSILS USED

IN THE MAKING OF CHINESE DISHES

A well-stocked Chinese kitchen usually has, besides a goodly collection of lidded pots and pans of varying sizes, several convex-bottomed circular pans hammered out of thin iron or copper called

Chinese *wock*

Wock 鑊 for the purpose of large quantity frying and braising. There are also different kinds of steamers; among these there is a lantern-shaped variety called *jing loong* 蒸 籠 steam lantern. It is a special contraption full of tiers of porous bamboo mesh-woven trays for the steaming of *deem sum* and a type of popular bread called *bow* 飽. Most *Daai See Foohs* simply use an ordinary large pot for steaming. A small can or pot is perforated with holes and

inverted in boiling water up to about three fourths of its height.
The dish containing the ingredients to be steamed is balanced upon

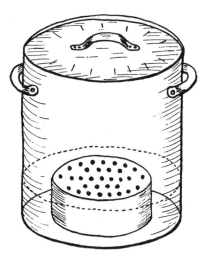

A homemade steamer

this inverted pot, the lid of the steamer is tightly placed upon the
pot, the heat is raised until the water reboils, and then the heat
is turned down, for rapidly boiling water does not give much more
heat than plain boiling water, but does raise your fuel bill.

Cleaver

Chopping and cutting are done with cleavers of varying sizes.
For mincing, a pair of cleavers of equal weight and size should be

used. Small cleavers for women's use generally have blades about 3 inches wide and 6 to 8 inches long. The blunt edge at the top of the blade is anywhere from $^1/_{16}$ to ⅛ of an inch wide. The edge of the blade is kept at razor sharpness.

The *jum baahn* 砧板 "chopping-block," for heavy chopping, mincing, and boning, is generally a smooth-surfaced section of the bole of a tree. It has a diameter of about 12 to 15 inches, and its height is about 6 to 8 inches. Mincing to a pulp and light slicing are done on an ordinary cutting board, which may be purchased under the name of bread board.

Chopping-block

A large smooth-surfaced pastry board is a must in a Chinese kitchen. It is about 22 inches by 28 inches and has two projections running along the length of the board. One projection is to keep the board steady against the table as you work the dough for homemade noodles, *Wun Tun* 雲吞 Cloud Swallows (see page 65), and other pastry dishes. The other projection keeps the flour from spreading messily off the area of the board.

The rolling pins are simple wooden rollers about 1 ¼ inches in diameter and anywhere from 8 to 30 inches in length. If you are honored by the presence of a *Daai See Fooh* in your home, don't be surprised when you find your brand new broom or mop handle mysteriously diminishing, or else profit by his example, as sections cut from these wooden poles and sandpapered to a high polish make excellent pastry rollers.

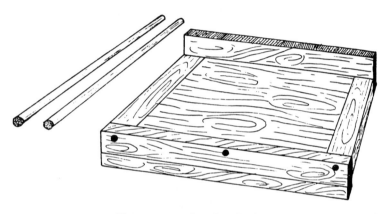

Chinese pastry board and rollers

Wocks and *jing loongs* are unpractical luxuries in the compact modern kitchen of today. As long as you have a fair collection of lidded pots and pans of varying sizes and depths, you will be able to prepare all the recipes given in this book.

Among the lighter utensils, you should try to have a set of hollow-ground knives. They are a blessing in the kitchen, are easy to handle, razor sharp, and wonderful for paper-thin slicing, paring, and cutting. It is also a good idea to obtain some wooden ladles or spoons if you are unable to handle bamboo or wooden chopsticks with agility, because it is best not to touch precooked food too much with metal implements. For deep-fat frying one should have a metal spoon perforated for the grease to drain through.

Light cooking utensils

Two heavy crockery jars should be kept in cool dark places to restrain the strained oils and drippings from cooking and deep-fat frying. Vegetable oils and drippings from lard, meat, or poultry should not be poured into the same jars. Oils and fats in which fish or sea food with strong odors have been fried can be reused after purification.

Several tight-lidded glass jars should be on hand for storing surplus vegetables, sauces, or other ingredients suspended in liquid that come from cans or bottles. These should then be kept in the warmest part of the refrigerator. Grains and dry ingredients must be kept in tight-lidded cans or bottles in dark, dry, and cool storage areas. The contents should be inspected at intervals.

HOW TO PLAN A CHINESE MEAL

If maximum preparation of ingredients before cooking is absolutely necessary to create a good meal, sensible planning of a menu is of equal importance. In the modern kitchen, with its usual limitations of space, time, the facilities of one's own hands, and the use of a four-to-six-range stove, one must plan a meal which can be cooked without confusion and the resulting frustration and nervousness. The experienced cook does not attempt to produce a dinner that will completely satisfy everyone's individual whims, but logically chooses a few practically managed dishes to revolve around the choicest of the recipes most in demand. He is also careful to make his selection from varying types of main ingredients, thus delicately balancing the final meal so that it consists of a seafood, poultry, meat, and vegetables.

Until one has become very expert, it is a mistake to attempt a meal of more than five dishes, including rice and soup. In planning the final menu, one must also take into consideration the elements of time and space, especially if the guests are known to linger over numerous "last cocktails." It is important not to choose more than one last-minute braised or fried dish; otherwise the strain of preparing and serving your masterpieces just done and piping hot will be too great.

With a four-range stove, two ranges are automatically utilized by the rice and soup. A third range should be used for a slow-cooking dish, which may be prepared early and more or less forgotten until needed. The fourth range should be kept in reserve for the last-minute braising of prepared ingredients for an instantaneous cooked dish. The fifth choice on the menu should be that of a roasted, grilled, or barbecued meat or poultry, for they, like the slow-cooking dish, can be more or less let alone until the last moment once the heat is properly taken care of.

In moments of emergency when unexpected guests stay on to dinner or on gay evenings when an unpremeditated dinner is suddenly decided upon, a most succulent meal may be served with very, very little effort. There is an easy and indescribably delicious sauce, in which meat and poultry may be marinated before being cooked, which is guaranteed to arouse the praises of all and establish the reputation of even the veriest novice among cooks.

42

Meat and poultry prepared in this manner may be served as a main course in an occidental meal, or as a dish in a Chinese menu. This sauce is especially effective when used on pork spareribs, pork chops, beef steaks and fillet of beef, or tender young chickens chopped into large fricassee portions.

1½–2 lbs. pork spareribs, chops,	*1 clove garlic*
beef steaks, fillet of beef, or one	*2 lumps sugar*
young chicken	*¼ cup soya sauce*
2 thin slices fresh ginger	*¼ tsp. pepper*
⅛ tsp. salt	

Smash ginger slices and mince very fine or to pulp if possible. Toss into glass and add sugar. Smash clove of garlic and mince until fine or to pulp. Add to sugar and ginger and crush all together until sugar lumps are crumbled. Add soya sauce, pepper, and salt. Stir well and then allow sauce to stand at least 10 minutes.

If steaks and fillet of beef are used, be sure that the individual portions are cut across the grain, pounded very, very lightly with the blunt edge of a knife, and rubbed with sauce. Cook in your favorite manner. If pork chops or chicken is used, merely rub the surface with the sauce and then roast or grill it in an oven set at 350° to 375° until done. And, if pork spareribs are used, take a sharp knife and cut the spaces between the ribs until almost through, rub the sauce thoroughly over the entire surface and into the cracks, and roast the meat in an oven at about 375° for about an hour.

Chinese meals are extremely elastic in relation to the number of persons to be served. The following sample menus will serve six to eight persons amply; and, if a couple of unexpected guests happen to appear on the scene, they may be welcomed without fears as to lack of food: just add extra places at the table and serve a larger quantity of rice.

Menu I: Chinese Cabbage Soup
Rice
Barbecued Spareribs
Pea Sprouts Braised With Pork
Curried Chicken

Menu II: Abalone Soup
Rice
Fried Shrimp Curls
Casserole of Mushrooms Squabs
Lima Beans Braised With Pork

Menu III: Lettuce and Fish Soup
Rice
Clear Steamed Chinese Mushrooms
Sweet-Sour Chicken Livers
Casserole of Five-Flowered Pork

Menu IV: Melted Asparagus Soup
Rice
Sweet-Sour Pungent Fish
Chicken Walnuts
Yang Chow Lion's Head

CHINESE DINNERS AND TABLE UTENSILS

CHINESE dinner parties are divided into two types, the informal, which is called *been faahn* 便飯 easy rice, meaning "meal without ceremony," and the formal, which is called *jow jick* 酒席 wine banquet. The formal term for such banquets is really *yin jick* 延席.

With informal dinners, the soup is placed on the table and then dinner is announced with the host and hostess urging the guests into the dining room, saying, "*Hoy Faahn, Luh! Chang Yup Luy, Aaah?*" 開飯喇 請入來 "The rice is opened! Please come in,

44

Uuuh?" * No one seems to hear the first summons or to move; after much additional urging on the part of the hosts, everyone rises together, but not a soul stirs. Polite gesturing is now the rule among the guests, each begging the other to precede him into the dining-room. The problem is eventually resolved and the guests trickle towards the table. The host and hostess sit together in the seats of least importance, with their backs nearest to the door; the guest of honor and his wife are placed directly opposite, with the other guests being seated according to their importance, until the least important finds his place next to the hosts.

As was mentioned above, the soup begins an informal dinner, or *been faahn;* following the soup, from four to eight dishes are placed on the table at the same time, together with the rice. Sometimes four large dishes are served consecutively and then four smaller *faahn choy* dishes are served as accompaniment for the rice. At a Chinese meal, dishes are never passed; the first helping is served to the guests by the host or hostess. Later, the host usually invites all to help themselves, saying, *Chûy been, chûy been, aaah?"* 隨便隨便 which means, more or less, "Just help yourself, no standing on ceremony."

Because dishes are usually never passed, Chinese prefer circular tables which allow for greater ease in boarding-house reaching and stretching. The ladies usually concentrate on the dishes directly in front of them or else just sit back and allow the gentlemen to serve them. In this way they manage to receive all the dainties, for who would serve others, especially ladies, anything but the choicest tidbits?

The host and hostess invariably start the meal by offering apologies for the insignificant display of dishes and their inferior qual-

---

* In China the staple food is rice, and the opening of a pot of rice by lifting its lid indicates that a meal is in readiness for serving. All other dishes are called *faahn choy* 飯菜 "rice-accompanying dishes," whose purpose is *soong faahn* 餸菜 "to send off the rice."

ity, which is unworthy of being served in the presence of such esteemed guests. The usual remark is, *"Dûy mmmm jüh, laah! Jun huy mo yeh seck."* 對唔住咯! 真係冇嘢食 "Please excuse me! There is really nothing to eat!" As a guest you are supposed to stare in bewilderment (which is generally quite genuine anyway) at the piled-high platters and protest violently, giving all the reasons why each dish is a masterpiece.

To exemplify the difference in customs between East and West, an occidental host is likely to be noisily proud of the specialties he has been able to procure for his guests, and quite frankly brags about each dish with such minute descriptions, whether true or not, that the diners are reduced to a state of semi-collapse by the time they are allowed to sample these vaunted masterpieces. The Chinese host, however, shows his good manners by profuse apologies for the food. It is up to the guest to refute these apologies energetically by praising all the virtues of the food with mouth-watering eloquence.

These simple differences in customs can lead to surprising complications. A well-known Chinese general was once host to many celebrated western guests at a famous restaurant in Paris. The dinner was ordered days in advance, and the chefs slaved to achieve the most succulent of exquisite masterpieces. The maitre d'hotel proudly led a file of dignified waiters parading around the table to display each dish with dramatic flourish, whereupon the host, with all his conservative Chinese good manners, embarked on an apologetic discourse. The guests perked up their ears and listened, first with incredulous surprise, then with growing sympathy, and soon with rapidly diminishing appetites. The maitre d'hotel upon overhearing the discourse became both indignant and unhappy, but the cooks were even more miserable. They thought that their hard-earned reputation had been ruined in an evening. Alarming complaints from the management and chefs rained upon the poor general, who was astonished to discover what an ungrate-

ful creature he was and at a loss to account for the minor catas-
trophe occasioned by his (Chinese) good breeding.

The formal Chinese banquet consists of a minimum of thirty-
two varieties of dishes, not counting such staple foods as rice, con-

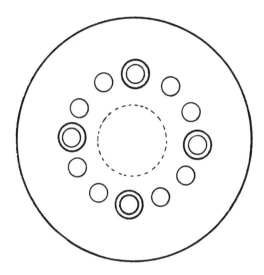

Arrangement of *wuy deep* on table

gee, or mien. Twelve cold dishes, called *wuy deep* 圍碟 "surrounding dishes," are placed decoratively in a circle on the table.
They are left there throughout the meal, but moved further away
from the center of the table when the main courses are served.
Four of these *wuy deep* consist of fruits, chiefly segmented citrous,
candied fruits, or some simple type of canned or fresh fruit like
pineapple and grapes. Four other dishes hold nuts, nut meats,
dried *luy jee* 荔 枝 "lichi nuts," or melon seeds. Another four dishes
hold such things as ancient eggs, sweet-sour pickles, slices of giblets, or slices of chicken and ham.

When the guests enter the dining-room, the host raises the con-

47

tainer of wine and fills the cups of the guests of honor, calls out their names, and invites them to take their indicated seats. Then he fills the other cups, in turn calling each guest, in accordance with his rank, to his seat. When everyone is placed, the host,

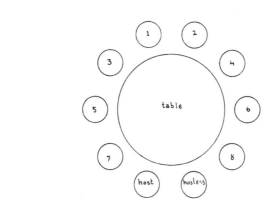

Chinese table seating

whose duty it is to start the drinking and eating, proceeds by lifting his cup to toast the guests and to invite them all to drink. The guest of honor usually invites the other guests to return a toast to the host and hostess. At the end of the dinner, hours later, the guests drink a toast of thanks to their host and hostess. Hot tea is served throughout the meal from beginning to end. After the wine toasts, everyone partakes of some of the tidbits, lively chatter is exchanged and all patiently wait for the main courses to come to the table.

Eight large dishes are served consecutively, two large dishes alternating with two smaller varieties. As a dish comes to the ta-

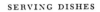

SERVING DISHES

Small dish   Large dish

ble, the host lifts his cup, inviting all to drink before sampling the new delicacy.

The first of the large dishes usually contains shark's fin, and the second another luxury, bird's nest soup. The seventh large dish consists of an elaborate dessert, and this is generally accompanied by four varieties of *deem sum* 點 心 appetizers (see page 56). The eighth and last large platter holds a steaming duck. To accompany this dish and those following, a guest's individual preference of rice or congee is served. And so the feast wends its way toward completion.

At both formal and informal dinners, as each guests eats his fill, he puts his chopsticks together, and gesturing with them to the others that he is through eating, urges them to continue with the words "*Maahn maahn*" 慢 慢 which mean more or less, "Please take your time and enjoy your meal."

Everyone is always gay and at ease throughout *been faahn*, but formal dinners are at times inclined to languish, especially after the third hour, when a full stomach and drowsiness begin to overcome one.

49

The dishwasher is always happy at the thought of Chinese *been faahn,* for there is comparatively little for him to do after a meal. The *Daai See Fooh* is accustomed to washing and putting away all of his utensils as soon as he is through with each, and as far as the table service is concerned very few utensils are used. Each person's place is set more or less as follows: a medium plate, a bowl for soup and rice, a saucer, a porcelain spoon, a pair of chopsticks, and a tiny tea cup. Sometimes a change of bowls is made when the

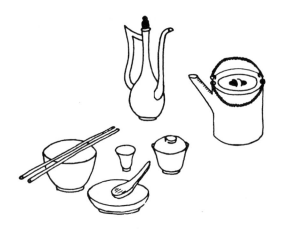

Table utensils

rice is brought to the table, but usually people just use their empty soup bowl and fill it with rice. Serving spoons and chopsticks are nowadays very often placed strategically close to each dish for hygienic reasons.

Chopsticks in South China are called *faai jee* 筷子 quick little boys. The name is probably derived from the fact that nibleness and speed of hand are needed in manipulating them. "Chopsticks" is the pidgin English translation of *faai jee.* "Chop chop" in pidgin English means "quick, quick," thus *faai jee* came to be called "Chop Sticks."

50

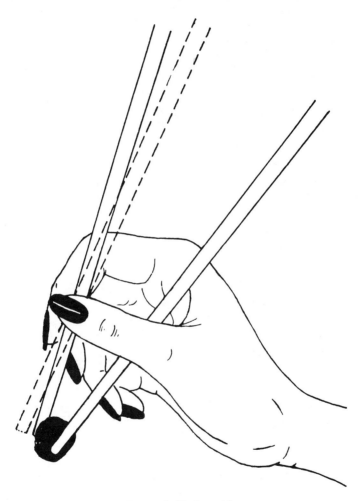

How to hold chopsticks

To manipulate chopsticks one must keep in mind that one stick always remains stationary, and the second acts as a lever which rises to encompass the food, and then is lowered until it grips the food firmly. The stationary stick is held between the thumb and the base of the index finger, and is supported by the last knuckle of the fourth finger. The second chopstick, which acts as a lever, is held pressed between the tip of the thumb and the cradle formed by the crooked first and second knuckles of the index finger. The third finger supports this chopstick and is also the power which moves it up or down.

Most people, when learning, attempt to pick up everything, without discriminating between dull-surfaced objects, elusive slippery objects, or such indefinite loose particles as mixed vegetables or rice. One can grip the first object squarely between the chopsticks, but one must lift up the elusive objects and the foods that come in loose particles. The latter motion is done by sliding the chopsticks under the objects and more or less scooping them up.

Chopsticks are made of bone, bamboo, wood, ivory, and, nowadays, even of plastic. Bamboo and wooden sticks are used in the kitchen for they withstand high temperatures and cause no changes in the taste of the cooking food. To the Chinese, ivory chopsticks at the table are like heavy sterling silverware to the westerner. However, great care must be given ivory chopsticks. They should not come in contact with extreme heat, for they will warp and also turn unpleasantly yellow or brown. Ivory chopsticks should be washed in sudsy lukewarm water and dried thoroughly.

If there are many superstitions concerning rice bowls, there are almost as many dealing with chopsticks. Thus, to drop them means bad luck, and to find a pair unmatched in length at your place at dinner means that you will miss your train, ship, or plane.

Chinese spoons are made of porcelain. Porcelain, unlike metal, does not conduct heat, nor does it change the taste of delicate foods. Thus one may drink relatively hot soup or liquids with a

Chinese spoon without burning one's lips and one may also taste the pure flavor uncontaminated by metal.

Most Chinese porcelains derive their shape from various fruits such as peaches, gourds, and pomegranates; or, like the wine jug, from the female form. These adapted forms may be plain or elaborately decorated.

The oldest and largest porcelain manufacturing city of China is Ching-Tê-Chên, near Kiu-Kiang. The potter's wheel was invented in China, and there from time immemorial the finest porcelains have been formed, decorated, and fired. The highest quality material used is *baak dun jee* 白墩子 a hard, white, fusible quartz. *Go ling* 高嶺 another excellent material, is composed of felspar or granite.

Perfection in porcelain is judged by the fineness of the material, the whiteness, and the glaze. If there are paintings, they must be well defined and sharp, with colors clear, clean, and well registered. The glaze must be brilliant and free of flaws. Most important of all, however, whether the chinaware is decorated or not, it must possess perfect harmony of form.

EQUIVALENT WEIGHTS AND MEASURES

3 teaspoons	1 tablespoon
4 tablespoons	¼ cup
16 tablespoons	1 cup
½ cup	1 gill
4 gills	1 pint
2 cups	1 pint
4 cups	1 quart
2 pints	1 quart
4 quarts	1 gallon
8 quarts	1 peck
4 pecks	1 bushel
16 ounces	1 pound
1 catty	1⅓ pounds
1 kilogram	2.2046 pounds
1 kilogram	1000 grams
1 tablespoon (liquid)	1 ounce
2 tablespoons (lard)	1 ounce
2 tablespoons (granulated sugar)	1 ounce
4 tablespoons (flour)	1 ounce
2 cups (minced meat)	1 pound

CANTONESE PRONUNCIATIONS

AA	as in	father, arm
ANG	,, ,,	hang, sang
AW	,, ,,	author
EE	,, ,,	feeble
EH	,, ,,	care
EUNG	,, ,,	e (eel) + u (fur) + ng (sing)
GW	,, ,,	Gwendolyn
I	,, ,,	fiasco, depend
IE	,, ,,	team, lean
IEU	,, ,,	dew, few
ING	,, ,,	ring, king
NG	,, ,,	sing
O	,, ,,	low
OO	,, ,,	tool
ON	,, ,,	gone
OY	,, ,,	coy, joy
OW	,, ,,	cow, now
ü	,, ,,	über, grün (German)
U	,, ,,	upper, come
UEN	,, ,,	u (unite) + e (end) + n
UK	,, ,,	hook, cook
UY	,, ,,	u (up) + y (sky)
ÜY	,, ,,	u (fur) + y (sky)

Chapter II

APPETIZERS

THE Chinese word for appetizer is *deem sum* 點心 which means "touch the heart." The term is derived from the fact that these dainties are served in small but satisfying amounts whenever the heart and stomach most crave them. Unlike occidental appetizers, *deem sum* are not usually eaten before a principal meal, but more frequently taken as a mid-morning, afternoon, or *sieu yeh* 宵夜 "through the night" snack.

There are both sweet and salty varieties of *deem sum,* and people love them for their extreme delicacy of flavor. In fact, so great is the popularity of these tidbits that many restaurants serve only this specialty during and around the hour of the noonday meal.

Sou Gock   Flaky Pastry

Two types of dough are needed in the making of this pastry. First prepare a large pastry board, a small rolling pin, and flour for dusting the board surface and the rolling pin. Next prepare all the ingredients needed to make the pastry.

Dough No. 1

2 *cups flour*   ¾ *cup strained suet*

Sift flour onto pastry board and blend in strained suet *(jüh yow)*. Knead delicately until dough is saturated with melting suet. Cover dough with slightly moist cloth until ready to use. Take care not to overhandle dough.

Dough No. 2

4 *cups sifted flour*   ½ *cup strained suet*
¼ *cup sugar*   1½ *cups water*

Sift 3 cups flour onto pastry board and keep one cup in reserve. Make a hollow in middle of pile of flour by stirring away flour with hand. Toss in sugar, 1 cup water, and creamed strained suet. Blend and knead lightly with fingers, adding water until all flour is included in the sticky marshmallow-like dough. Then add enough flour so that when kneaded in firm push-away and pull-up and fold-back motion consistency will change to that of firm marshmallow, nonadhering to the fingers, and extremely elastic. Care must be taken not to overwork dough. Cover dough with moist cloth if you are not ready to use it immediately.

Roll Dough No. 1 into narrow sausage about ½ inch in diameter, and then cut off sections about ½ inch long.

Roll Dough No. 2 into sausage about 1 inch in diameter, and cut off sections about ½ inch long. There should be an equal number of pieces from each of the doughs.

Flatten piece of Dough No. 2 with fingers, and place piece of Dough No. 1 in center. Draw up Dough No. 2 on all sides and thoroughly envelop Dough No. 1 by pinching all seams firmly and then rolling ball between palms of hands. Place ball of doughs, welded side down, on flour-dusted surface of pastry board. When all pieces have been used up, there should be about 50 balls of dough.

Dust pastry board lightly, place on it a ball of dough, welded side down, and roll out firmly in thin narrow length about 6 inches or more. The longer you roll the length, the flakier the pastry will become. Starting from one end of length, curl up dough into a roll, loop one end of dough-roll under, and then loop other end under the first. Stand folded dough upon pastry board, smooth hump side up. Repeat procedure with all remaining balls of dough.

To shape pastry into turnovers, take a looped roll of dough, place smooth hump side up on pastry board, and roll into thin pancake about 3 to 4 inches in diameter. Place ball or heaping tea-spoon of filling in center, and fold pancake over into semicircle. Pinch edges together into ½-inch-wide ledge, and then form scroll design along arc of turnover. To form scroll design, hold arc of turnover toward you. Starting from left hand side, push up a bit of ledge at an angle, press down fold; push up some more ledge, press down fold; and repeat process until scroll design extends all the way along arc (see illustrations).

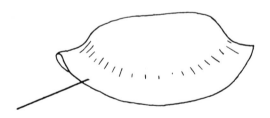

A.—Pinch edges of dough to form ledge for turnover scroll design

Either bake filled turnovers 20 minutes or fry in hot deep fat to a rich golden hue. Care must be taken that deep fat is not too hot, for then pastry will expand too rapidly, shatter, and turn bitter-brown on outside, but remain raw on inside. If oil is not hot enough, turnovers will become soaked with grease and become indigestible.

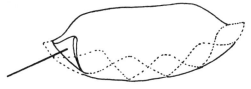

B.—How to begin and continue scroll design

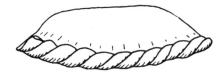

C.—Turnover with scroll edging

To shape the pastry like Parker House rolls, dust pastry board lightly, place on it lump of folded dough-roll smooth hump side up, roll dough into pancake 2½ inches in diameter, place lump of sweet filling or generous teaspoon of salty filling in center, bring up sides of pancake, and entirely envelop filling. Be sure that seams are tightly sealed. Roll ball gently between palms of hands, place seams side down on pastry board, roll ball into 3-inch pancake, turn pancake over and double into semicircle. Bake in moderate oven about 15 to 20 minutes.

鹹 酥 角 心

Haahm Sou Gock Sum

Salty Flaky Pastry Filling

1 cup fresh shrimps
½ cup minced pork
2 slices smoked ham
2 slices smoked bacon
½ cup bamboo shoots
4 Chinese mushrooms, soaked
3 scallions

6 stems parsley leaves
1 tbls. cornstarch
1 tbls. soya sauce
½ tsp. salt
½ tsp. sugar
½ tsp. pepper
2 tbls. sesame seeds

1 tbls. salad oil

Chop shrimps; mince pork, ham, bacon, bamboo shoots, Chinese mushrooms, scallions, parsley; and mix ingredients thoroughly in bowl. Add cornstarch, soya sauce, salt, sugar pepper, and salad oil. Blend into mixture and allow to soak. Toast sesame seeds to a golden color over extremely low fire and add to mixture. Heat a little oil in pan and then fry ingredients until cooked.

One generous teaspoon of this filling is the average amount for one turnover or Parker House roll.

豆 沙 角

Dow Saah Gock

Sweet Bean Filled Pastry

If you cannot purchase sweet bean filling called *dow saah* 豆 沙 in any of the Chinese grocery shops or restaurants, prepare your favorite nondripping gooey tart or pie filling or use the one described below:

2 lbs. honey dates   *½ cup powdered sugar*
¼ cup creamed butter

Pit dates and mash to fine pulp. Blend in ¼ cup creamed butter and ½ cup powdered sugar. Roll mass into sausage about 1 inch in diameter; cut off sections about ¾ inch in length. Roll each piece into ball and use as sweet filling for either turnovers or rolls in shape of Parker House rolls.

Gow Jee   Transparent Dumplings

1 lb. dung fun *(pure wheat flour*   *3-4 cups boiling water*
which becomes transparent)   *¼ cup salad oil*
Important! Short finger nails.

Place *dung fun* 澄 粉 in pot, stir in 3 cups boiling water with wooden stick, and blend mixture until consistency resembles that of firm, semitransparent, but nonadhering paste. Add more boiling water if necessary. Cover pot with lid and let dough bake in its own heat.

Bring out pastry board, and place dish of salad oil within easy reach. Have moist cloth and cleaver in readiness. Oil surface of board and your palms and fingers; place dough on board and start kneading in a strong pushing-and-pulling motion. Dip hands in oil frequently because the oil prevents sticking. When dough has become elastic, roll into loaf and cut in two with oiled blade of cleaver. Store one half of dough in pot and cover pot firmly with lid. Roll other half into sausage about 1 inch in diameter. Oil blade of cleaver and cut off pieces about ¾ inch long. Cover pieces with damp cloth. Take each piece and roll into ball; then placing ball close to edge of pastry board, press several times with oiled blade of cleaver until it becomes a pancake about 3½ inches in diameter. Put 1 heaping teaspoon filling in center of pancake and fold dough into bonnet-shaped pouch (see illustrations).

A.—How to fold bonnet-shaped pouch

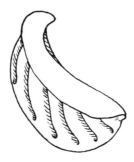

B.—Bonnet-shaped pouch

To form bonnet-shaped pouch, keep side of semicircle facing you smooth. Crook index finger of right hand against the dough on opposite side (which will eventually form the pouch side), and with index finger of left hand, push dough partly over the crooked finger of right hand in deep crease. Remove crooked finger of right hand and press folds together at top, close to the edge. Continue process 6 to 7 times until end of the arc is reached. Now press ledge into thin rim. The entire pouch should remind you of a wide-brimmed bonnet. Repeat process until all dough is used up. Makes about 24 *Gow Jees.*

Now paint skins of the *Gow Jees* with a little salad oil, steam for 15 minutes and serve piping hot.

While one lot of *Gow Jees* is steaming, take up remaining half of dough in pot and repeat process.

炸 餃 子

Jaah Gow Jee   Fried Transparent Dumplings

Use the same dough recipe as in Transparent Dumplings. The only difference is in the manner of wrapping in the filling. The procedure is very similar to that of making Flaky-Pastry turnovers (page 58).

After rolling individual pieces of dough into balls, press each with blade of cleaver into pancake about 2½ inches in diameter. Pick up pancake and press middle area thinner than outer edge by pressing pancake between thumbs and forefingers. This procedure increases diameter of pancake about 1 inch; it also gives pancake a slight concavity.

Place generous teaspoon of filling or ball of filling in center of concave pancake. Fold pancake over to form semicircle, and press edges together until thin ½-inch ledge is formed. Face arc of semicircle toward you and starting from left-hand corner push up ledge at an angle at the corner; press fold lightly; and repeat process until entire scroll pattern is formed along arc of semicircle.

Heat about 1 inch of oil in shallow skillet, place *Gow Jees* in delicately, and fry 3 to 4 minutes on each side, or until golden brown. Serve hot.

豆 沙 餃 子

Dow Saah Gow Jee   Sweet Bean Filled Dumplings

1 cup dow saah *filling*   ½ recipe gow jee *dough*
(makes about 24)

Roll *dow saah* (see page 60) into sausage about ¾ inch in diameter. Cut sausage into ¾-inch lengths. Roll each piece of *dow saah* into a ball.

Prepare *gow jee* dough as usual (see page 61) but wrap Sweet Dumplings in the same manner as Fried Dumplings; that is, resembling a turnover with a scroll. Oil surface of each turnover and place on tray in steamer to steam for 20 minutes. Serve piping hot.

鹹 心 餃 子

Haahm Sum Gow Jee   Stuffed Salty Dumplings

1 got (*Chinese turnip-like root vegetable*)°
½ lb. loin pork
½ cup shelled shrimps
2 slices smoked bacon
2 slices smoked ham
1 small piece bamboo shoot
½ cup parsley stems and leaves

3 scallions
4 Chinese mushrooms
2 tbls. cornstarch
1 tbls. soya sauce
1 tbls. salad oil
1 tsp. sugar
1 tsp. salt
½ tsp. pepper

Mince-dice got 薯, pork, shrimps, bacon, ham, bamboo shoot, parsley, scallions, and mushrooms. Mix ingredients together in

° Jícama may be substituted for *got*.

64

bowl and flavor with sauce made of cornstarch, soya sauce, salad oil, sugar, salt, and pepper. Allow flavor to seep into ingredients for about ½ hour before using as filling.

Prepare *gow jee* dough as usual (see page 61) but wrap filling in bonnet-shaped pouch. Paint skins lightly with salad oil, gently place each *gow jee* tray in steamer and steam for 15 to 20 minutes. Serve piping hot.

Wun Tun   Cloud Swallows

Before giving the recipe for *Wun Tun*, I should like to mention that *Wun Tun* skins may be purchased ready made at certain Chinese grocery shops and restaurants. The homemade variety, however, if made like that of the *Daai See Fooh*, is delicious. For the novice, making *Wun Tun* requires time, patience, deftness, and perseverance; but practice in this case really brings facility and perfection.

PROCEDURE

First have in readiness one large pastry board about 22 inches by 28 inches, two rolling pins about 30 inches in length, and a cheesecloth bag containing 1 to 2 cups cornstarch for dusting dough and pastry board.

2 cups flour		*1 teaspoon salt*
	3 eggs	

Sift flour and salt in heap in center of pastry board. Stir with fingers at center heap to form a hollow and break eggs into it. Stir

65

and knead with fingers until all flour is included in dough. A little water may be added if absolutely necessary, but dough should be an adhering mass and yet as stiff and dry as possible. Shape dough into a neat loaf and then start kneading hard. The more you knead the more elastic the dough, and the better the *Wun Tun*. So knead hard and firmly with the balls of your palms in strong push-away, pull-up, and fold-over motion until dough gains smoothness and elasticity. When dough is thoroughly kneaded, roll back into neat loaf and cover with moist cloth until ready to use.

Now scrape surface of pastry board clean and dust thoroughly with cornstarch, which should be at hand in cheesecloth bag. Then, using rolling pin, roll out loaf of dough into as long a ribbon as possible. Dust ribbon of dough and wind onto one of the rolling pins. Then repeat actions No. 1 and No. 2 (indicated) until dough is as wide° as or even wider than pastry board's length. The dough should also be so thin and transparent that the grain of the wood in the pastry board can be clearly seen through it. The thinner the dough, the better the *Wun Tun*. This recipe will make around 100 squares of skins.

Action No. 1: Draw out rolling pin from roll of dough, and proceeding from center of roll, work toward end pressing rolling pin down on roll of dough firmly and evenly with an outward motion. Repeat process on other half of dough-roll. This procedure increases the width and thinness of the dough tremendously.

Action 2: Unwind flattened and broadened dough-roll, about 8 inches at a time. Dust surface thoroughly with cornstarch, roll dough thinner with rolling pin, dust dough generously again, and wind dough onto second rolling pin. Continue process until all dough is wound onto second rolling pin.

° Since it is difficult for the novice to roll the dough smoothly and evenly as soon as it begins to acquire width, cut the dough-roll in half when it begins to get out of hand. Cover one portion of dough-roll with a damp cloth and continue working with the other half first.

Repeat Actions No. 1 and No. 2 until dough is thin and transparent enough. End with dough wound up on a rolling pin. Lift rolling pin with its mass of dough about 6 inches, and, unwinding dough gradually, weave rolling pin back and forth so that dough falls upon itself in layers about 2½ inches wide (see illustration).

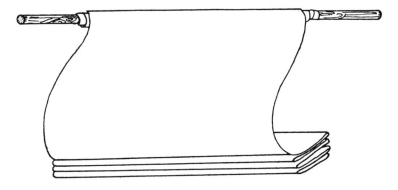

Wun tun dough being folded in layers

When all dough is thus folded, take sharp knife and cut pile into squared-off sections of 2½ inches by 2½ inches. Take sections, unwind into lengths of ribbons, and lay on top of each other. Using knife again, cut off squared-off sections so that skins are 2½ inches by 2½ inches. Now you have little piles of square semitransparent dough, which are called *wun tun pay* 雲 吞 皮 Wun Tun "skin." If skins have tendency to stick to each other,* loosen by grasping center of pile between thumb and forefinger and shaking whole pile hard. Cover skins with moist cloth until you are ready to use them.

* Skins have a tendency to stick only if the dough was too moist or if insufficient cornstarch was used during the preparation.

HOW TO WRAP WUN TUN

Take a square of *Wun Tun* skin, scoop up ⅓ teaspoon filling with point of chopstick, and place filling on one corner of square (the one closest to you). Now, with chopstick in place, roll up *Wun Tun* skin toward opposite corner, and take out chopstick. Place pin point of filling on surface of one of two ends of *Wun Tun* roll, double the other over to cover pin point of filling and then pinch the two ends together. Now wrapped *Wun Tun* should look like a Chinese imperial goldfish with graceful flickering fins, or like little wisps of fleecy clouds.

Chicken *Wun Tun* Filling

½ lb. chicken fillet °	1 tsp. sugar
2 scallions	1 tsp. cornstarch
¼ cup parsley leaves	1 tbls. soya sauce
1 slice ginger	¼ tsp. pepper
1 tbls. vegetable oil	½ tsp. salt

Mince chicken, scallions, parsley leaves, and ginger. Add sugar, salt, pepper, cornstarch, oil, and soya sauce. Allow mixture to soak about ½ hour.

° Pork or shrimps may be used in the recipe instead of chicken.

鶏湯雲吞

Ghuy Tong Wun Tun   Velvet Chicken Broth Wun Tun

1 chicken carcass   ½ teaspoon mei-jing (gourmet
1 cup fillet of chicken   powder)
1 slice smoked ham   1 tsp. soya sauce
6 Chinese mushrooms   1 tsp. cornstarch
4 stalks celery   ½ tsp. sugar
2 tbls. salt   1 tsp. oil
                    ¼ tsp. pepper

Dump chicken carcass into 3 quarts water. Bring water to boil and add salt. Simmer for 3 hours and then pour broth through sieve into fresh pot. Slice ham, mushrooms, and celery, and add to broth. Slice chicken fillet very fine and add ½ teaspoon salt, sugar, pepper, soya sauce, cornstarch, and oil. Allow mixture to soak 15 minutes. Then add to simmering soup along with the *mei-jing*.

Drop into large pot of boiling water as many *Wun Tun* as you wish to serve, allow to boil 2 minutes, drain in colander, and then drop into soup. Simmer another 5 to 10 minutes and serve. Garnish surface with minced smoked ham and Chinese parsley leaves.

炸 雲 吞

Jaah Wun Tun   Fried Wun Tun

Heat about 1 inch of vegetable oil in skillet, put in wrapped *Wun Tun* and fry to rich golden taffy color. Pierce each with colored toothpick and serve. Fried *Wun Tun* are excellent for cocktail parties. Serve hot.

Another delicious way of eating Fried *Wun Tun* is as an accompaniment to such pungent dishes as sweet-sour spareribs or chicken livers and giblets.

Chün Gün

Spring Rolls

Since the real Chinese method of making Spring Rolls wrapping is a simple-looking feat which frustrates and bring tears of wrath to every amateur, *Daai See Foohs* have smugly condescended to think up some methods which will allow the novice peace of mind and successful results. The genuine method of the experts is to mix flour and water until a consistency of elastic marshmallow is reached. This mass is then allowed to stand about 10 or 15 minutes. In the meanwhile a greasy smooth surface like that of a griddle plate is warmed up. A mass of dough is taken in the hand and pressed against the warmed surface. A thin filmy sheet of dough should be left on the surface, which, when dried, should resemble a delicate sheet of rice paper about the size of the palm of the hand. Below, I shall give two simpler methods of making *Chün Gün* wrappings.

Chün Gün No. 1

Spring Roll No. 1

Make a *Wun Tun* dough (see page 65). When semitransparent and delicate enough so that the grain of the wood of the pastry board may be seen through it, cut dough into 6-inch squares. Cut each square diagonally in half. Place generous tablespoon of filling along base of triangle, allowing about ¾ inch of edge. Fold this edge over stuffing, bring the two points over sufficiently to keep in the stuffing securely, and then bring apex of triangle over to close package. Place each oblong Spring Roll package carefully on greased steaming tray. Do not let Spring Rolls touch each other at this stage or they will stick together. Steam each trayful about 10 minutes. Then fry in hot deep fat until rich golden-brown color is acquired. Serve with lemon, lime, or mustard.

Filling for Spring Roll No. 1

2 scallions	6 water chestnuts
1 cup parsley leaves	6 Chinese mushrooms
¼ lb. loin pork	½ tsp. sugar
4 slices smoked ham	1 tbls. soya sauce
½ lb. shelled shrimps	¼ tsp. pepper
1 lb. pea sprouts	2 tsp. cornstarch
½ cup bamboo shoots	¼ cup vegetable oil

2 tsp. salt

Slice scallions down the center and chop fine diagonally. Fine-dice pork, ham, and shrimps. Wash pea sprouts and simmer 2 minutes in boiling water. Add teaspoon salt, drain off boiling water, rinse rapidly with cold water, and then allow pea sprouts to cool. Slice bamboo shoot, water chestnuts, and Chinese mushrooms into thin matchsticks. Chop parsley leaves. Toss all ingredients into large bowl and then add sugar, soya sauce, pepper, cornstarch, vegetable oil, and salt. Mix everything together thoroughly.

Chün Gün No. 2   Spring Roll No. 2

1 cup flour	½ teaspoon salt
2 eggs	2 cups water

Sift flour into bowl and blend in eggs, salt, and enough water to make the mass a smooth thin batter. Beat batter in one direction only to gain elasticity.

Lightly grease flat-surfaced pan about 6 inches in diameter, and warm on lowest heat. Beat batter again, and then pour 1 tablespoon batter into pan. Allow batter to spread over entire surface and set into sheer, flexible, very thin pancake. When it shrinks away from bottom of pan, turn pancake over to dry and set a little

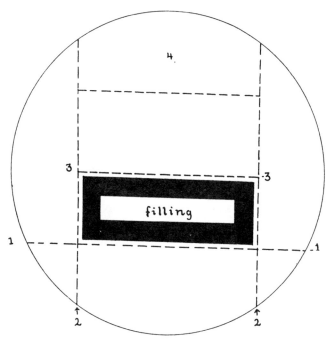

How to fold *chün gün* No. 2

on other surface. Do not let pancake get too dry. As each pancake is ready, remove to dish and cover with moist cloth until you are ready to use it.

To wrap Spring Rolls No. 2, place 2 tablespoons chilled *Chün Gün* filling on each pancake (see illustration). Spread filling out lengthwise and fold in pancake envelope fashion. That is, first fold over flap along length of filling, then fold over two flaps along sides of filling, last of all moisten edge of remaining flap and seal filling up in a *Chün Gün* envelope.

Heat about 1 inch of vegetable oil in deep skillet and fry Spring Rolls until skins are rich golden-taffy color. Drain and serve hot with lemon slices, lime slices, or English mustard.

Spring Roll Filling No. 2

½ lb. fillet of chicken, or canned crab meat, or pork, or shrimp meat	2 cups spinach leaves
	1 tbls. soya sauce
2 scallions	1 slice ginger, minced
4 Chinese mushrooms	1 tsp. cornstarch
2 cups pea sprouts	½ tsp. salt
½ tsp. sugar	

Shred fillet of chicken (or crab meat). Mince shrimps (or pork) and add cornstarch, salt, sugar and 1 teaspoon soya sauce. Chop scallions, slice mushrooms thin, break pea sprout stems and spinach leaves in halves. Heat a little oil in skillet, fry scallions lightly, and then add pea sprouts, spinach leaves and 2 teaspoons soya sauce. Fry together 2 minutes and remove to dish. Heat a little oil in skillet, fry minced ginger, and then add chicken mixture. Fry chicken mixture 1 minute and add cooked vegetables and fry together another 2 minutes. Allow *Chün Gün* filling to cool before attempting to wrap in skins. If time permits, chill filling before using.

Chapter III

CHINESE SOUPS

ALL Chinese soups 湯 *tong* are delicious. Yet most Chinese soups are made within half an hour. There are some soups of course, like the shark's fin soup, which may take anywhere from to three to five days to cook, but this book will deal chiefly with a number of soup recipes that ought to cheer every busy housewife's heart, and are made in the "quick soup" manner. In this type of soup, beneficial elements and vitamins from the vegetables and meats are retained; and, as for the vegetables and meat, they remain fresh, and extremely tasty and tender.

Baak Choy Tong   Chinese Cabbage Soup

1 head Chinese cabbage	½ tsp. cornstarch
2 ounces lean pork	2 tsp. soya sauce
1 tablespoon salt	½ tsp. sugar
2 slices ginger	¼ tsp. pepper
1½ quarts boiling water	½ tsp. mei-jing powder
1 tsp. vegetable oil	

Slice lean pork fine and mix with sugar, pepper, soya sauce, cornstarch, and vegetable oil. Heat a little oil in pot (just enough to grease bottom of pot), fry ginger and salt for ½ minute, and then pour in 6 cups boiling water. Slice cabbage coarse and add to boiling soup. Cover pot with lid and simmer 10 minutes. Add pork mixture and *mei-jing* powder. Cover pot with lid and allow soup to simmer 10 to 15 minutes more.

生 菜 魚 湯

Saang Choy Yü Tong   Lettuce and Fish Soup

1 *head lettuce*	1 *tbls. soya sauce*
¼ *lb. fillet of fish*	1 *tsp. cornstarch*
2 *slices ginger*	½ *tsp. sugar*
2 *tsp. salt*	½ *tsp. pepper*
6 *cups boiling water*	1 *tbls. vegetable oil*

1 *tsp.* mei jing *powder*

Slice fillet of fish and add cornstarch, soya sauce, sugar, pepper, and oil. Separate the leaves of lettuce. Pour the very minimum of oil into a pot to heat, and then fry ginger slices and salt for ½ minute. Pour in boiling water, bring to quick boil, toss in lettuce, simmer 5 minutes with lid on, toss in fish mixture and *mei-jing* powder and simmer 5 to 10 minutes more.

75

鷄 肝 湯

Guy Gon Tong   Chicken Liver Soup

1 cup chicken livers, hearts, and gizzards	3 pints boiling water
	1 tbls. soya sauce
1 head Chinese cabbage, or 1 lb. spinach	½ tsp. sugar
	1 tsp. cornstarch
1 generous slice ginger	1 tbls. vegetable oil
2 tsp. salt	½ tsp. pepper

Slice gizzards into flowers, that is cut into pieces and then cut parallel rows of lines into surface. Next cut perpendicular rows of lines across first lines. Mix gizzards, hearts, and liver with soya sauce, sugar, cornstarch, vegetable oil, and pepper. Heat a little oil in a pot, and fry ginger and salt for ½ minute. Add 6 cups boiling water. When water is swiftly boiling again, add coarsely sliced cabbage and chicken liver mixture. Cover pot with lid and simmer slowly 20 to 30 minutes.

西 洋 菜 湯

Suy Yeung Choy Tong   Watercress Soup

1 lb. watercress	1 tbls. soya sauce
¼ lb. lean pork	1 tsp. cornstarch
2 slices ginger	1 tbls. vegetable oil
1 tbls. salt	½ tsp. sugar
3 pints boiling water	½ tsp. pepper

Slice pork fine and mix with cornstarch, sugar, pepper, soya sauce, and vegetable oil. Heat a little oil in a pot, fry ginger and salt for ½ minute, and then pour in 6 cups boiling water. Bring water to swift boil, add watercress, cover pot with lid, and simmer 5 minutes. Add pork mixture and simmer another 10 to 15 minutes.

Gwaah Jee Choy Tong   Chinese Watercress° Soup

1 lb. gwaah jee choy (*Chinese watercress*)
2 ounces minced pork
2 slices ginger
1 tbls. salt
3 pints boiling water

1 tsp. cornstarch
1 tbls. soya sauce
½ tsp. sugar
½ tsp. pepper
1 tbls. vegetable oil
2 well-beaten eggs

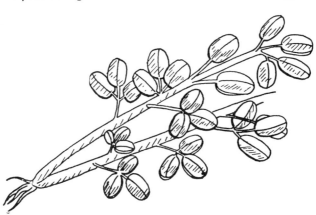

Chinese watercress

° *Gwaah jee choy*, Chinese watercress (see illustration), called *verdolagas* in Mexico, has a slight vinegar flavor. Its leaves resemble the shape of watermelon seeds, and thus in China it has acquired the name of "Melon seed plant." Unlike the watercress, *gwaah jee choy* seems to be a padded plant saturated with water.

77

Mix minced pork with cornstarch, sugar, pepper, soya sauce, and vegetable oil. Heat a little oil in a pot, fry ginger and salt for ½ minute, and pour in 6 cups boiling water. Bring water to fresh boil and toss in Chinese watercress, cover pot with lid, and simmer 10 minutes. Then toss in meat mixture. Cover pot, boil 5 minutes, take pot off fire and allow soup to cook in its own heat for 5 minutes. Stir in beaten eggs gently, and when eggs are slightly set, serve.

鮑 魚 湯

Bow Yü Tong   Abalone Soup

4 Chinese mushrooms	2 teaspoons salt
½ small can abalone	1 tsp. cornstarch
4 stalks celery	1 tbls. soya sauce
2 slices smoked ham	½ tsp. sugar
2 ounces lean pork	1 tbls. vegetable oil
2 slices ginger	½ tsp. pepper

6 cups boiling water

Slice Chinese mushrooms and celery. Cut ham and abalone into matchsticks. Slice pork and mix with cornstarch, soya sauce, sugar, oil, and pepper. Heat a little oil in a pot, fry ginger and salt for ½ minute, and then pour in 6 cups boiling water. When water reboils, add mushrooms, celery, and pork mixture. Cover pot with lid and simmer 10 minutes. Add ham and abalone, simmer 5 minutes, and serve. Do not overcook abalone, for it then becomes tough and rubbery.

78

泰米蛋花湯

Sook Muy Daahn Faah Tong	Fresh Corn Egg Flower Soup

4 *stalks fresh corn cob*	1 *tbls. vegetable oil*
¼ *onion*	1 *tbls. salt*
1 *scallion bulb*	½ *tsp. pepper*
1 *clove garlic*	½ *tsp. sugar*
1 *slice ginger*	1 *tbls. soya sauce*
¼ *lb. lean pork*	1 *tbls. cornstarch*
3 *eggs*	6 *cups boiling water*

Mince pork and add cornstarch, oil, sugar, pepper, soya sauce, 2 tablespoons water, and ½ tablespoon salt. Use sharp knife and scrape all corn kernels into bowl. Mince ginger, garlic, onion, and scallion.

Heat a little oil in a pot, and fry ginger, onion, garlic, scallion, and salt. After 1 minute, add 6 cups boiling water and then corn kernels. Cover pot with lid and bring soup to boil, and then let simmer 10 minutes. Add meat mixture, cover, and simmer another 10 minutes. Take pot off the fire, and remove lid. Beat eggs and stir into soup.

蓮藕湯

Lien Ngow Tong	Lotus Root Soup

1 *section lotus root stem*	2 *thick slices ginger*
½ *lb.* ngow baak naam (*beef plate*)	2 *tbls. cooking sherry*
1 *piece* gwaw pay (*dried tangerine skin*)	2 *tbls. salt*
6 hoong joe (*dried Chinese dates*)	½ *tsp. pepper*
	¼ *cup vegetable oil*
3 *quarts boiling water*	

79

Place meat in pot of cold water with 1 teaspoon salt, and bring water to boil. Take out meat and throw away water. Cut beef into 1 inch cubes. Heat oil in pot, and fry ginger with 1 tablespoon salt for 1 minute. Add diced beef, wine, 1 tablespoon salt, and pepper, and brown meat slightly. Add 3 quarts boiling water. Cover pot with lid and bring soup to boil, then let simmer slowly. Slice lotus root diagonally, and together with red dates and tangerine skin (*gwaw pay*) add to soup mixture. Simmer soup slowly at least 3 hours.

猪 脚 腐 竹 湯

Jüh Gerk Fooh Jook Tong   Pig's Feet Soya Bean Soup

4 *pig's feet*	1 *tbls. sherry*
6 ho-see (*dried oysters*)	2 *tbls. salt*
6 *pieces* fooh jook (*bean curd*)	1 *small piece ginger*
6 hoong joe (*dried Chinese red dates*)	1 *tsp.* mei-jing *powder*
	3 *quarts boiling water*

Pour boiling water over pig's feet and let them soak 20 minutes. Then chop into large pieces. Place dried oysters in hot water, bring water to boil, allow oysters to soak 10 minutes and then clean thoroughly. Soak *fooh jook* about ½ hour.

Heat a little oil in a pot, fry sliced piece of ginger and salt a minute, then toss in sherry, soaked oysters, and pieces of pig's feet. Fry until pig's feet are a rich golden hue, then pour in 3 quarts boiling water. Cover pot with lid and allow soup to simmer. Add *hoong joe,* and *fooh jook* cut into 2-inch pieces.

Allow soup to simmer 4 hours. Half an hour before serving soup, add *mei-jing* powder.

燉 白 鴿

Dun Baak Gup   Broth of Pigeon

            2 fat squabs   2 tbls. sherry
            1 lb. winter melon meat   1 tbls. soya sauce
            4 large Chinese mushrooms   2 tsp. sugar
            2 slices ginger   1 tbls. salt
            2 scallions   ¼ cup salad oil

Cut rind off winter melon and slice meat into ¼-inch thick pieces. Sprinkle melon with salt and fry in 1 tablespoon salad oil for 2 minutes. Remove melon to small but tall pot. Split squabs in two along spine, then brown in remaining oil after rubbing with soya sauce. Add browned squabs to fried melon, add mushrooms, finely sliced ginger, chopped scallions, sugar, sherry, and enough water to cover generously (about 2 quarts).

Place narrow tall pot in a yet taller and larger pot. Fill space in between with enough boiling water to reach one third to one half the height of inner pot. Cover outer pot with lid and bring water to simmer. Simmer 2 to 3 hours or until squabs are tender. A young chicken cut into pieces makes a good substitute.

雞 蓉 露 笋

Ghuy Yoong Low Sün   Melted Asparagus Soup

            2 cans white asparagus   2 slices smoked ham
            2 pieces breast of chicken   ¾ cup cornstarch
            1 carcass of chicken   2 tbls. salt
            5 egg whites   1 tsp. mei-jing powder
                        4 quarts boiling water

81

Heat 1 tablespoon of oil in a large pot and fry salt. Pour in 1 gallon boiling water and toss in chicken carcass. Cover pot with lid and simmer three hours. Strain soup into a fresh pot. Take out 1 cup of broth and chill it.

Open cans of asparagus. Keep only ½ cup juice. Using sharp knife, slice asparagus open and scrape out delicate portions of stem and tip into a pulp. Throw away fibrous outer-end portions. Mix juice with scraped asparagus pulp.

Mince chicken breasts and then pound to pulp with blunt top edge of cleaver. Mix chilled chicken broth gradually into chicken pulp. Beat mixture with chopsticks or fork, beating in one direction only. Every now and then remove the mass of muscle and sinew strands clinging to chopsticks. When there are no more strands of muscle or sinew, beat egg white until frothy and add to chicken purée. Dissolve cornstarch in cold water.

As soon as broth reboils in fresh pot, add asparagus pulp and 1 teaspoon *mei-jing* powder. Then slowly and carefully stir in cornstarch mixture. Simmer for 15 to 20 minutes, add salt to taste, and then beat mixture of chicken and egg white. Turn off fire and allow chicken to cook in heat of soup for 5 to 10 minutes. In the meanwhile, mince ham and use it over soup as garnish.

Doong Gwaah Joong   Winter Melon Pond

1 tender winter melon about 1 foot tall by 8 inches wide	2 pairs chicken breasts
½ cup lien jee (lotus seeds)	2 pieces smoked ham
6 Chinese mushrooms sliced	1 tbls. sherry
¼ cup abalone diced	1 tsp. sugar
½ cup bamboo shoots diced	1 tsp. salt
1 slice ginger	¼ tsp. pepper
	1 chicken carcass

Simmer chicken carcass in 2 quarts water for 3 hours. Cut ¼ off length of winter melon, scrape bowl of melon clean of pulp and seeds. Tie heavy string loosely around melon in the form of a basket (see illustration). Set winter melon in pot which fits its circumference. Set the whole in larger pot for steaming. Fill space between pots with boiling water until water level reaches seven

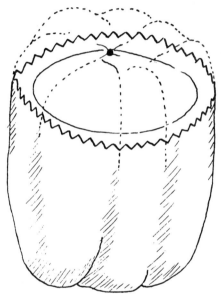

How to prepare winter melon pond

eighths the height of inner pot. Strain chicken broth into winter melon pond until it is two-thirds full. Add 1 teaspoon salt and cover outer pot with lid.

Boil lotus seeds 10 minutes and clean them of their brown husks. Add lotus seeds and sliced mushrooms to winter melon pond. Steam about 5 hours or until winter melon meat is transparent and tender.

In the meanwhile, dice chicken breasts and mix with sherry, sugar, salt, and pepper. Heat a little oil in a tiny tall pot, fry minced ginger and chicken until slightly browned. Pour in 1 pint strained chicken broth. Place smaller pot in larger pot, fill space in between with enough water to generate steam. Cover outer pot firmly with lid and allow contents to cook 3 to 4 hours. Pour this concentrated soup into winter melon pond.

Five minutes before serving, add fine diced ham, bamboo shoots, and abalone to pond. Also add *mei-jing* powder and salt to taste. Lift melon pond out of container carefully by strings and lower it gently into attractive serving bowl. Cut strings away and serve winter melon pond.

魚 肚

Yü To   Fish Tripe

Dried fish tripe 魚 肚 *yü to* comes whole in a large flat piece, which is generally about 18 inches by 8 inches. It is the color of parchment. Soak *yü to* in cold water for about 20 minutes, then place in an oven in low heat for about ½ hour or until edges begin to curl together. Now with sharp knife cut the large piece of *yü to* into squares about 1½ inches by 1½ inches. Place squares on baking sheet and bake in low oven until they puff up high and look like large toasted buns about 2½ inches by 2½ inches by 2½ inches in size (takes about 1½ hours). These *Yü To* buns may be cooled and then stored in an airtight can for future use.

In order to use *Yü To* buns for cooking, take about one fourth of the buns and soak overnight in cold water. By the next day they will have doubled their volume and will look like smooth-coated gelatinous sponges. Cut off all smooth gelatinous skins with pair of shears, leaving only porous white mass, which is then cut into quarters and soaked in fresh cold water. Squeeze several times and then squeeze out as much water as possible. Place drained sponges in dry bowl and pour 2 tablespoons sherry over them. Squeeze wine into sponges and allow wine to seep in for 15 minutes. Then squeeze sponges as dry as possible again. Sprinkle *Yü To* sponges with ½ teaspoon pepper and 1 tablespoon of your finest sherry. Now the *Yü To* may be added to clear soup.

清 湯 魚 肚

Ching Tong Yü To   Clear Broth Fish Tripe

¼ *of* yü to *buns*   *2 slices smoked ham, julienned*
1 chicken carcass   ¼ *cup diced bamboo shoots*
4 Chinese mushrooms sliced   ¼ *tsp. pepper*
2 tbls. salt   *1 tsp.* mei-jing *powder*
                        8 sugar peas (Chinese peas)

Simmer carcass, neck, and wings of chicken for 3 hours in 4 quarts water. Add 2 tablespoons salt. Strain broth into fresh pot, add mushrooms, ham, bamboo shoots, pepper, *mei jing, Yü To* sponges (see page 84), and simmer 30 minutes. Serve. If Chinese peas are used for decorative garnish, simmer them 15 minutes.

鷄 蓉 燕 窩

Ghuy Yoong Yien Waw   Swallow's Nest Soup

1½ oz. dragon's teeth (dried swal-   *3 egg whites*
    low's nest°)   *2 tbls. cornstarch*
2 qts. chicken broth   *2 tsp. salt*
1 pair chicken breasts   *2 slices smoked ham*

° *Yien waw*  "swallow's nest" (popularly known as bird's nest) of

Soak dried swallow's nest chips in 1 pint boiling water overnight. Place the resulting expanded gelatinous mass in sieve and drain off water. Place the now separated transparent gelatinous shreds in pot with 3 cups hot water and simmer ½ hour. Remove the transparent mass to a bowl to cool.

In the meanwhile prepare sufficient chicken broth by cooking up all chicken bones, neck, and lower legs and wings. Simmer at least 3 hours with about 2 teaspoons salt. Drain broth into fresh pot. Take out 1 cup to chill.

Mince chicken breast meat into pulp, stir chilled broth slowly into this mass of pulp, and continue stirring with fork or pair of chopsticks until all sinews and strands of muscles cling around prongs of fork or tips of chop sticks and can be removed. Beat 3 egg whites into chicken pulp "melt."

Add swallow's nest to chicken broth 15 minutes before serving. Stir cornstarch with a little water and add to broth. Add salt to taste. Just before serving, take simmering thickened soup off fire and slowly stir in "melt" of chicken and egg white. Pour soup into attractive bowl and garnish with minced ham. Serve.

the finest quality usually comes in two forms: as cleaned and purified dried cuplike nestlets, or cleaned and purified dried slightly curved chips called *loong ngaah* 龍 芽 "dragon's teeth." Each box usually contains 6 ounces of dried swallow's nest gelatinous protein. 1 to 1½ ounces of this will serve 6 to 8 people generously.

Chapter IV

EGG DISHES

THE egg is the embodiment of the symbol of *yeung* and *yum*, which represent the negative and the positive principles of universal life. The yolk and the white are likened to the darkness and the light of the two principles. *Yeung* 陽 is the essence of the positive forces of the heaven, the sun, the light, vigor, the male, penetration, and the monad. *Yum* 陰, as its antithesis, represents the negative forces of the earth, the moon, the darkness, quiescence, the female, absorption, and the duad. The circle embodying the two principles, like the egg shell, signifies the origin of creation, which when divided into its two primary constituents forms the male and the female. From the union of these two, five virtues should evolve: benevolence, purity, propriety, wisdom, and truth.

Nutritiously speaking, eggs are interesting and valuable as food since they embody all the elements necessary to the development of life. Eggs, like milk, constitute a complete food. Even as far back as the eleventh century, the structure of the egg attracted enough attention so that a treatise was written on the subject by the eminent poet genius Su-Tung-Po 蘇東坡 (1036-1101). Throughout the pages the manner of boiling eggs so that the albumen hardens in separate layers is explained in detail.

Careful examination of the egg reveals many interesting factors hidden beneath its porous shell. The rich yolk is held within an extremely delicate membrane, which suspends it protectively inside layers of albumen. The egg white usually consists of four layers; the innermost one is watery, the next two are jelly-like, and the fourth outermost layer is again watery. The egg white is protected from the entrance of foreign material through the porosity of the eggshell by a membrane.

粉 絲 猪 肉 炒 蛋

Fun See Jüh Yook Daahn   Cellophane Noodle Eggs

¼ lb. minced pork	½ tsp. sugar
½ tbls. soya sauce	1 stalk celery
1 tsp. cornstarch	3 scallions
1 tbls. salad oil	¼ cup parsley leaves
¼ tsp. pepper	1 generous fistful of fun see (powdered silk)
½ tbls. salt	
1 slice smoked ham	6 eggs
1 tsp. mei-jing powder	

Mix pork with soya sauce, cornstarch, salad oil, ½ teaspoon salt, pepper, and sugar. Chop celery, scallions, and parsley. Allow *fun see* to soak in boiling water until tender. Beat eggs and add 1 teaspoon salt and *mei-jing* powder. Slice ham into matchsticks.

Heat a very little salad oil in a pan, toss in vegetables and fry a moment. Add pork mixture and ham and fry a while. Add *fun see,* mix thoroughly, cover skillet with lid, braise mixture 2 minutes. Pour in beaten eggs and scramble on low fire until eggs begin to set but are yet a bit liquid. Remove pan from fire, scramble until eggs reach the stage of being merely extremely moist. Remove to a dish and serve.

Jing Daahn   Steamed Egg Custard

4 eggs   1 pint stock or hot water
4 stalks scallions   ½ tsp. salt
2 tsp. soya sauce   ¼ tsp. pepper

Chop scallions, including most of green leafy portion. Beat eggs, and add salt and pepper, then stir in hot water or stock. Pour into attractive serving dish, sprinkle with scallions, and steam 15 to 20 minutes. Sprinkle with soya sauce and serve.

In making steamed custards, always use hot liquids with eggs, for this results in creamy textures, whereas cold liquids cause air-holes and unevenness.

荷 包 蛋

Haw Bow Daahn   Coin Purse Eggs

2 eggs per person   Vegetable oil
Salt   Soya sauce
Pepper   Sprigs of parsley

Heat ⅛ inch of oil in pan with concave base. Carefully break 1 egg in center of pan. Sprinkle with salt and pepper. When egg white has congealed below but upper surface is yet moist, flip one half of egg over the other half to form semicircle. Fry egg on both sides until done and then place carefully and neatly on attractive serving dish. Repeat process with remainder of eggs. The important thing to remember is to keep heat low during cooking and then raise it when egg has been folded and is well under control. This raising of heat gives the outer surfaces a nice rich golden color. Now sprinkle all eggs with a little soya sauce and garnish dish with sprigs of parsley.

The eggs derive their name from their close resemblance to a coin purse. The egg white represents the purse, and the egg yolk within represents the golden coin.

Foo Yoong Daahn   Rich Egg Omelet

6 eggs	1 cup shredded pork, or crab, or
6 scallions chopped	shrimp, or chicken, or chaah sieu
2 cups pea sprouts	(barbecued pork)
¼ cup mince-diced smoked ham	1 slice ginger minced
2 Chinese mushrooms sliced	1 tsp. salt
1 stalk celery sliced thin	½ tsp. pepper

soya sauce to taste

Break pea sprouts in half. Heat a little oil in a pan and fry ginger, scallions, celery, pea sprouts, mushrooms, salt, pepper, ham, and pork (or other meat) until cooked. In the meanwhile beat eggs and then stir in cooked ingredients. Heat more oil in frying pan, pour in enough egg mixture to form small omelet, and fry on both sides until golden brown. Repeat process with rest of mixture. Garnish with parsley sprigs and sprinkle with soya sauce.

豌 豆 炒 蛋

Woon Dow Chow Daahn   Scrambled Eggs and Peas

1 cup fresh green peas   1 slice bacon
6 eggs   1 tsp. salt
1 scallion chopped   ¼ tsp. pepper
1 slice smoked ham   1 tbls. dry sherry

Boil peas with pinch of soda until tender, and remove outer skin of each pea, if you have the patience. Chop scallion, dice ham and bacon. Heat a little oil in a pan, fry scallion, ham, bacon, and peas; sprinkle with salt and pepper. Fry a few moments and stir in eggs. Add sherry if desired. When eggs begin to set but are yet extremely moist, remove from pan into serving dish. By the time eggs reach the table to be served they will have cooked themselves to the right consistency with their own heat.

鷄 蛋 餃

Ghuy Daahn Gow   Egg Pouch Omelet

4 eggs   1 tbls. vegetable oil
¼ lb. minced pork   ½ tsp. sugar
4 scallions chopped   ¼ tsp. pepper
2 tsp. soya sauce   1 slice ginger minced
½ tsp. salt   2 tsp. cornstarch
3 tbls. oyster sauce, ho yow

Mix pork with scallions, ginger, ½ teaspoon cornstarch, soya sauce, sugar, salt, pepper, and vegetable oil. Scoop out teaspoonfuls of mixture and place on platter within easy reach of stove.

91

Heat a little oil in a frying pan concave in the center. Beat eggs and carefully pour 1 tablespoonful into concave of pan to form tiny omelet. Immediately, while upper surface is still moist, drop 1 teaspoon of meat mixture in center of omelet and flip half of it over to form a semicircle pouch. Press edges together and remove pouch to dish. Repeat process until all are done, then place dish in steamer for 15 to 20 minutes.

In the meanwhile, make a sauce of ½ cup water, 3 tablespoons oyster sauce, and 1½ teaspoon cornstarch. Stir and simmer until thickened. Take egg pouches out of steamer, pour oyster sauce over them, garnish dish with sprigs of parsley, and serve.

Daahn Faah

Egg Garnish

3 eggs   ½ tsp. salt

Beat eggs and salt. Oil an 8 to 9-inch flat-bottomed pan slightly and warm over low fire. Pour one third of egg mixture into pan, and spread it all around evenly by tipping pan. Cook eggs over low fire until set. Spread this sheer omelet upon platter to cool. Repeat process with remainder of eggs.

To cut omelets into garnish, place omelets on top of each other, cut into 2-inch strips, pile strips on top of each other, and slice into ⅛-inch-wide lengths. Toss these short narrow strips around a little in order to disarrange them, and then sprinkle over dishes as garnish.

Pay Daahn   Ancient Eggs

This recipe is given only to satisfy your curiosity and solve the mystery which revolves around ancient eggs. The recipe comes from a very old cook book which counsels, "While making *pay daahn*, avoid strangers, shun too many people, especially friends and acquaintances, and do not gossip or talk more than is vitally necessary." Since I felt I should never be able to follow the rules, I have not tested the recipe.

1 *portion ashes of pine wood*	½ *portion lime*
1 *portion ashes of charcoal*	*duck eggs (fresh)*
1 *portion ashes from the kitchen stove*	⅛ *oz. salt per egg*
	Coarse cheap tea leaves

Take large quantity of cheap tea leaves and brew strong mixture. Mix this essence of tea with equal portions of ashes of pine wood, charcoal, stove, plus half a portion of lime. Add salt in correct proportion to eggs being cured. Now cover each egg with this claylike ash mixture. Do not skimp.

Line large earthenware container with earth. Carefully place coated eggs upon layer of earth. Allow 2 inches of space between each egg. Fill spaces in between eggs with earth. Also cover eggs with generous layer of earth. Place container in cool dark place and allow to cure for 100 days. During that time follow the rule of silence with strict attention.

Chapter V

FISH AND SHELLFISH

An early civilizer by the name of *Fook Hey* (about 2953 B.C.) is honored as being the person who taught the people of China the method of making fish nets and the finer techniques of fishing. During the Yin Period ° (1400 B.C.) improved methods of catching fish were recorded upon slips of bamboo and carved scapulae of animals in various forms of pictograms. Through these inscriptions we learn that the people of Shang † (1523-1027 B.C.) caught their fish not only with nets but also through the use of pole, line, and bait.

Owing to economic reasons, fish and shellfish have become two of China's principal food staples. The extensive coast line, swift rivers, enormous lakes, and great network of little canals in China serve as bountiful and happy hunting grounds for the fishermen. There are no restrictions as to seasons or the amount a person may catch, so fishing continues unhampered all the year round. At some fishing stations, the men are allotted certain areas, but they are not taxed except for the registration of their fishing vessels.

° *Yin* is pronounced *Yun* in Cantonese.
† *Shang* is prononunced *Sheung* in Cantonese.

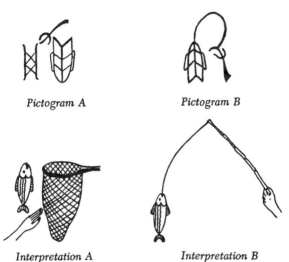

Pictogram A   Pictogram B

Interpretation A   Interpretation B

Pictograms of Sheung Period and their interpretations

The fish most eaten in China are: carp 鯉魚 *lay yü;* sea bass 海鱸魚 *hoy lo yü;* river bass 河鱸魚 *haw lo yü;* sea bream 大頭魚 *daai tao yü;* bream (blue-gill) 扁魚 *been yü;* bull-head (catfish) 大頭魚 *daai tao yü; cod* 魯魚 *lo yü;* herring 白魚 *baak yü;* minnow 小黄瓜魚 *sieu waung gwaah yü* (little yellow melon fish); mullet 黄花魚 *waung faah yü;* perch 桂魚 *gwuy yü;* sea perch 海桂魚 *hoy gwuy yü;* salmon 沙門魚 *saah mun yü;* shark-fin 魚翅 *yü Chee;* shad 鰣 *chieh yü;* tuna 金槍魚 *gum cheung yü;* snappers (red) 紅魚 *hoong yü;* sole (dabs) 尖魚 *jiem yü;* sturgeon 惠王魚 *wuy waung yü;* turbot 疕子魚 *ping jee yü;* mandarin fish 李花魚 *lay faah yü;* and whitebait 銀魚 *ngun yü.*

The shellfish most eaten are: shrimp 蝦 *haah;* prawn 大蝦 *daai haah;* crab 螃蟹 *pong haai;* lobster 北蝦 *loong haah;* clams 蛤蚧 *gup ghaai;* oysters 蠔 *ho;* bêche de mer (sea slugs) 海參 *hoy sum;* abalone 鮑魚 *bow yü;* and scallops 江瑤柱 *gon yiu chee.*

95

The Chinese word for fish 魚. *yü* resembles phonetically the word meaning "superfluity." Thus fish are used as a symbol for wealth and abundance. Fish generally swim in pairs within schools, and so they signify the joys and harmony of union, connubial bliss, and regeneration. Their movement of swiftly and sharply darting from any obstruction, their sensitiveness, their reckless and fearless perseverance in swimming against currents indicate freedom from restraint and distinctive courage.

In selecting fresh or frozen fish, always be sure that the fish has bright red gills, bright eyes that remain firm to the touch, firm elastic flesh, and a fresh odor. As soon as you get the fish home, clean and dress it, wash it under cold water rapidly, wipe it inside and out, sprinkle it lightly with salt, and place it in the coldest part of your refrigerator until ready to use.

In selecting lobsters that are uncooked, be sure to buy them alive. If you buy boiled lobster, be sure that it was alive prior to the moment of boiling. One can ascertain this fact by straightening the lobster's tail. If the lobster was alive before it was plunged into boiling water, its tail will spring back to its original position.

In selecting shrimps, see that the shrimps are firm of flesh and slightly bluish gray in color. As the shrimps grow less fresh, the color begins to turn to an opaquish white tinged with pink. Wash the shrimps and clean them as soon as you get them home. Always place them in the coldest part of your refrigerator until the moment you need them. Remove the black thread which runs along the back. This is the intestinal tract and imparts a sandy sensation which is quite unpleasant. If the recipe calls for shelling, remove the shell, but try not to knock off the tail. It acquires a bright red shade after cooking and adds color and cheer to the finished dish. If the recipe does not call for shelling, slit the shell along the black line with a very sharp knife and remove the grit. It is also advisable to cut off all the legs.

五 柳 魚

Ngung Lao Yü   Five Willows Fish

or

甜 酸 魚

Tiem Shün Yü   Sweet Sour Pungent Fish (popular name)

1 2-3 lb. red snapper   *2 cloves garlic*
1 firm cucumber   *2 tbls. sugar*
1 carrot   *½ cup vinegar*
1 piece young ginger   *1 tbls.* hoy sien jeung
1 sweet pickle   *2 tsp. cornstarch*
½ Spanish onion   *Salt*
                2 tbls. salad oil

Slice cucumber in two lengthwise, remove soft pulp, and then slice into 2-inch long matchsticks. Scrape carrot and slice into 2-inch long matchsticks. Slice young ginger and sweet pickle into needlelike sticks. Mince onion fine. Sprinkle 1 teaspoon salt over vegetables, let seep in for 10 minutes, and then add 4 to 6 teaspoons sugar, ½ cup vinegar, and ½ cup water. Allow ingredients to marinate about ½ hour.

In the meanwhile, heat 2 quarts water in large, flattish, lidded pot. When boiling, add 2 tablespoons salt and 2 tablespoons oil. Raise heat so water comes to rapid boil, place fish carefully in water, cover pot with lid, and then turn off fire entirely, thus allowing fish to cook in heat of water (about ½ hour).

Drain vegetables and place in dry dish. Make a sauce, using vinegar mixture in which vegetables marinated (add sugar to taste if necessary), 1 tablespoon *hoy sien jeung*, 2 teaspoons cornstarch

THE JOY OF CHINESE COOKING

dissolved in a little water. Heat a little oil in a pan, fry two crushed cloves of garlic, and then add sauce and simmer until it thickens.

If the fish is too cool after soaking, reheat rapidly in same water, take out, sprinkle lightly with salt and white pepper, then cover with layer of marinated vegetables, pour sauce over this, and then finally pour 2 tablespoons salad oil over sauce.

釀 魚

Yeung Yü   Stuffed Fish

1 large-boned 3 lb. fish	¼ tsp. salt
4 Chinese dried shrimps	¼ tsp. pepper
6 water chestnuts	½ tsp. sugar
4 Chinese mushrooms	1 tbls. soya sauce
2 sprigs parsley	2 tbls. water
1 slice smoked ham	2 tsp. cornstarch
3 scallions	1 tbls. salad oil

Grasp fish by tail, and working from tail toward head, use sharp knife and cut away flesh of fish from bone. Then with spoon or blade of knife, scrape flesh away from skin, taking great care to keep latter intact. Spread the two pieces of skin out on plate. Mince fish-flesh. Soak shrimps and mushrooms until tender and then mince. Dice fine water chestnuts and ham. Chop scallions and parsley. Mix all ingredients in bowl and add salt, pepper, sugar, soya sauce, cornstarch, salad oil, and water. Mix thoroughly and shape ingredients into neat mound on layer of fish skin. Flatten mound and cover surface with other layer of fish skin. Heat about ⅛ inch of oil in frying pan, and brown fish on both sides to rich golden shade.

In the meanwhile, make a sauce of the following:

2 tbls. sherry   1 tbls. soya sauce
1 tbls. sugar   1 slice minced ginger
                ½ cup water

Pour sauce over frying fish, cover pan with lid and braise fish for 3 minutes. Turn fish over carefully and continue braising about 15 minutes. Serve.

鷄 油 鯉 魚

Ghuy Yow Lay Yü   Chicken-Fat Braised Carp

1 3 lb. carp (or sea bass)   1 clove garlic
¼ cup chicken fat   2 tbls. soya sauce
1 tsp. salt   3 tbls. oyster sauce
1 tsp. sugar   2 tbls. Chinese chile sauce or
4 thin slices tender ginger   1 tbls. tabasco sauce
4 scallions   2 cakes fresh soya bean curd
            Unsalted chicken broth

Mince ginger and garlic, and chop scallions into 2-inch lengths. Sprinkle carp with salt and rub salt well into skin. Heat chicken fat in skillet, add chile or tabasco sauce and oyster sauce, toss in garlic, ginger, scallions, and sugar. When skillet is extremely hot, lay fish in and brown on both sides. Pour boiling chicken broth into skillet until level barely covers fish. Cover skillet with lid and simmer fish about 10 minutes or until fish is done. Remove fish carefully to dish. Add to sauce soya bean cakes which have been cut into pieces 1 inch by 1 inch by ½ inch and boil 10 to 15 minutes. Arrange bean curd around fish and pour simmering sauce over fish.

Jing Yü   Steamed Fish

1 medium-sized flat fish (sole or dab)	2 Chinese mushrooms
½ tsp. salt	1 dozen golden needles (gum jum)
¼ tsp. pepper	2 slices young ginger
½ tsp. sugar	1 scallion
2 tsp. cornstarch	1 thin slice smoked ham
2 tbls. soya sauce	2 dried Chinese dates (hoong joe)
2 tbls. vegetable oil	

Clean and wipe fish. Place in attractive little serving dish, sprinkle with ¼ teaspoon salt, pepper, sugar, 1 teaspoon cornstarch, 1 tablespoon soya sauce, and 1 tablespoon vegetable oil. Mix thoroughly and rub into fish.

Soak mushrooms, golden needles, and dates until soft, then slice mushrooms, ginger, and dates fine. Cut golden needles in half. Chop scallion and cut ham into matchsticks. Mix ingredients with ¼ teaspoon salt, pepper, sugar, 1 teaspoon cornstarch, 1 tablespoon soya sauce, and 1 tablespoon vegetable oil. Spread over surface of fish. Place fish in steamer and steam about 20 minutes.

Chow Yü   Braised Fish

1 1 lb. fish (whole)	1 tbls. soya sauce
1 tsp. salt	1 tbls. sherry
2 slices young ginger	¼ cup parsley leaves
1 tsp. sugar	3 scallions
½ tsp. pepper	

Mince ginger and crush into 1 teaspoon sugar. Add sherry, soya sauce, and enough water to make ½ cup sauce. Heat vegetable oil in pan and brown fish on both sides. Add soya sauce, cover pan with lid, and braise fish 10 minutes. Place fish in attractive dish, sprinkle with pepper, chopped scallions, and parsley leaves. Place in steamer and steam 5 to 10 minutes. Serve.

Baak Faahn Yü   White Upside Down Fish

1½ lbs. fillet of herring	½ tsp. salt
3 egg whites beaten stiff	¼ tsp. sugar
2 egg yolks	1 tsp. soya sauce
¼ tsp. pepper	tomato catsup

Beat egg yolks with pepper, salt, sugar, and soya sauce. Coat fish fillet with this yolk mixture. Heat vegetable oil in frying pan, lay fish fillet carefully in pan and fry one side until honey-golden hue. Turn fish fillet over, spread stiff egg white over all evenly, fry until base is golden-brown in color, and then skillfully turn entire contents of pan upside down so that egg white may acquire coat of golden tan. Fry 1 minute over very hot fire and then turn entire mass onto serving dish, egg white side up. Sprinkle catsup upon egg white in generous and decorative blobs. Serve.

HOW TO PREPARE MINCED FISH FOR STUFFING OR FISHBALLS

Grasp large boned fish by tail, then using sharp knife, work from tail toward head, cutting flesh of fish away from spine. Cut each fish fillet lengthwise in half. Holding each strip by skin, use sharp knife to scrape off flesh of fish. Gather all scraped fillet of fish and chop into fine mince. Place minced fish in large mixing bowl and add:

For each pound of minced fish
$\left\{\begin{array}{l}\text{¼ cup water} \\ \text{1 tsp. salt} \\ \text{1 tsp. cornstarch} \\ \text{½ tsp. sugar}\end{array}\right.$

Knead mass with hand and stir in one direction with firm motion until consistency of minced fish turns to that of soft marshmallow. Lift mass several times and thrust back strongly into mixing bowl (as if with vengeful vindictiveness). When mass loses quality of spattering as it hits base of bowl it is ready. This smashing and knocking the fish around gives it an adhering quality. As soon as the minced fish acquires this quality it may be used for stuffing or may be made into fishballs.

釀 瓜

Yeung Gwaah   Stuffed Braised Squash

    5 squash   ½ tsp. salt
    ½ lb. prepared minced fish   1 tbls. sherry
    ¾ cup hot water   soya sauce

If you are using the round variety of squash, merely cut squash into ¾-inch-thick slices. However, if you are using the long variety of squash, cut slices ¾-inch thick but slightly diagonally. Split each slice of squash in half almost to end, open up like oyster shells, and stuff opening with 2 tsp. minced fish. Makes about 20.

Heat a little vegetable oil in a skillet, fry stuffed squash fish side down until golden crust is formed. In the meanwhile, mix salt, soya sauce, sherry, and hot water into sauce and add to frying stuffed squash. Cover pan with lid and braise squash about 30 minutes or until squash is tender. Serve—fish side up upon the platter.

魚釀苦瓜

Yü Yeung Fooh Gwaah   Bitter Melon Stuffed With Fish

> 3 medium-sized bitter melons   1 tbls. dow see (black beans)
> ½ lb. prepared minced fish   1 clove garlic
>   ½ cup hot water

Cut bitter melons (balsam pears) into 1-inch thick disks. Using small knife, scrape out white pulp. Stuff hollowed-out disks of bitter melon levelly with minced fish. (Minced fish upon cooking has a tendency to expand — see page 102.) Heat a little oil in a skillet and fry both sides of flat stuffed disks until fish forms a golden crust.

Make a sauce of 1 tablespoon crushed dow see and 1 clove of crushed garlic. Add ½ cup hot water. Pour sauce over frying stuffed bitter melon. Cover skillet with lid and braise stuffed melon over low fire about 20 minutes.

清蒸冬菇

Ching Jing Doong Gwooh   Clear Steamed Chinese Mushrooms

> 24 Chinese mushrooms, well   1 tbls. dow see (black beans)
>   formed and medium sized   1 tsp. soya sauce
> 1 bunch Chinese parsley   1 tbls. vegetable oil
>   ½ lb. prepared minced fish

Soak medium-sized well-formed Chinese mushrooms 15 to 30 minutes. Clean thoroughly and carefully remove stems. Take 1 to 1½ teaspoons minced fish and form dainty mound upon each mushroom. Place sprig of parsley leaves upon each mound of fish so that it looks like peaked cap (leaves usually come in sprigs of three leaves). Place stuffed mushroom on attractive serving dish and steam about 30 minutes. Before serving, sprinkle stuffed mushrooms with soya sauce and cooked vegetable oil.

炒 鮑 魚 片

Chow Bow Yü Pien   Braised Abalone

½ can abalone (½ lb.)	½ cup Chinese peas (mange tout)
1 clove garlic	4 leaves Chinese cabbage
2 slices ginger	1 tbls. soya sauce
½ cup sliced bamboo shoots	2 tbls. dry sherry
2 slices smoked ham	2 tsp. cornstarch
½ Spanish onion	½ tsp. sugar
2 stalks celery	½ tsp. pepper
2 Chinese mushrooms	1 tsp. salt

Slice abalone into thin sheets and cut into medium-sized pieces (roughly ⅛ inch by 1 inch by ½ inch). Cut cabbage and smoked ham into matching slices. Slice onion, celery, bamboo, mushrooms into fine slices. Heat a little oil in a pan and fry all vegetables with salt for ½ minute. Cover pan with lid and braise vegetables 5 to 10 minutes. Remove to dish. Add a little more oil to frying pan, toss in smashed garlic and ginger, and then abalone. Fry a few seconds and then return vegetables and stir in sauce made of sherry, cornstarch, soya sauce, pepper, and sugar. Cover pan with lid and braise ingredients for 3 minutes. Serve. Care must be taken not to overcook the abalone.

蠔油鮑魚片

Ho Yow Bow Yü Pien   Oyster Sauce Braised Abalone

1 can abalone   ¼ cup abalone water
¼ cup oyster sauce   1 tsp. soya sauce
1 tbls. cornstarch   1 slice smoked ham
               1 sprig parsley

Dice the abalone into pieces about 1 inch by 1 inch by ½ inch.
Heat a little oil in pan, toss abolone in and stir around for ½
minute. Then sprinkle with oyster sauce, soya sauce and cornstarch dissolved in abalone water, and fry 2 minutes more, stirring
constantly. Turn out upon attractive dish, sprinkle with minced
smoked ham and decorate further with sprig of parsley in center.
Serve immediately. Take care not to overcook abalone, for then
it becomes tough and rubbery.

芽菜炒蝦

Ngaah Choy Chow Haah   Pea Sprouts Braised With Shrimps

1 lb. pea sprouts   1 clove garlic
1 cup shelled shrimps   1 tbls. soya sauce
½ cup Chinese peas (mange tout) 1 tsp. salt
½ Spanish onion   1 tsp. sugar
¼ cup cloud ears (wun yee)   ½ tsp. pepper
3 stalks celery   2 tsp. cornstarch
2 slices ginger   1 tbls. dry sherry

Slice onions, ginger, and celery fine. Chop up shrimps roughly.
Heat a little oil in a frying pan and fry onions, Chinese peas, celery,

pea sprouts, and a sprinkling of 1 teaspoon salt. Braise well until tender but yet crisp (about 3 minutes). Remove to dish. Add a little more oil to frying pan, toss in smashed clove of garlic and minced ginger. Add shrimps and braise 1 minute. Add all vegetables and then cornstarch mixture consisting of soya sauce, pepper, sugar, sherry, 1 tablespoon water, and cornstarch. Blend ingredients thoroughly, cover pan with lid and braise 2 to 3 minutes. Turn out on dish and serve.

炒 蝦 碌

Chow Haah Look   Fried Shrimp Curls

1 lb. shrimps with shells	1 piece ginger
3 tbls. hoy sien jeung	1 clove garlic
2 tsp. sugar	½ tsp. pepper
2 tbls. vinegar	1 tsp. salt
6 scallions	1 tsp. cornstarch

½ tsp. soya sauce

Wash shrimps in cold water in which salt and baking soda have been dissolved. Drain, pull off legs. Place shrimps in dish and sprinkle with pepper. Make sauce of hoy sien jeung, sugar, ½ tsp. salt, and vinegar. Chop the scallions into 1-inch lengths and mince garlic and ginger. Heat a little oil in a frying pan, fry shrimps 1 minute on each side, sprinkle with ½ tsp. salt, and add scallions, ginger, garlic, and sauce. Fry and stir, and then add a mixture of cornstarch dissolved in water and soya sauce. Braise shrimps 2 minutes more and serve.

茄汁炒蝦球

Keh Jup Chow Haah Kow   Tomato Braised Shrimp Balls

3 lbs. fresh shrimps	12 scallions
4 eggs	6 celery stalks
3 tbls. cornstarch	2 green bell peppers
4 tsp. sugar	2 red bell peppers
1 tbls. salt	4 Chinese mushrooms
2 tbls. soya sauce	4 slices smoked ham
1 tbls. vegetable oil	6 large red ripe tomatos
2 cloves garlic	1½ tsp. pepper

Wash shrimps in salt water and bit of baking soda. Shell shrimps and mince. Add eggs, 2 tablespoons cornstarch, 1 teaspoon pepper, 1 tablespoon sugar, 1 tablespoon soya sauce, 2 teaspoons salt, 1 tablespoon oil. Stir mixture with your hand in one direction until mixture is well blended. Pick up mound and slap back into mixing bowl until mixture stops splattering when it hits base of bowl.

Heat about 4 inches water in large pot to boiling point. Take handful of shrimp mixture and squeeze about 1 teaspoonful through the hollow between the thumb and the base of the index finger. Break off this little mass and drop into boiling water. Cover pot with lid; when balls float to surface and are pink, white, and gold in color, they are ready. It is best to do the shrimps in three or four batches. Drain each lot after cooking, allow them to cool, and place in large dish.

Cut the scallions and celery into 1-inch lengths. Quarter bell peppers, remove seeds and membranes, and cut peppers into rectangles ½ inch by 1 inch. Slice ham and mushrooms coarsely. Mince garlic. Scald tomatos, peel, and mince to pulp. Heat a little oil in a large skillet, fry garlic, bell peppers, and celery. Add 1 teaspoon salt and ½ teaspoon pepper. Cover skillet with lid and braise ingredients 2 minutes. Add scallions, then braise ingredients another 1 to 2 minutes. Add shrimp balls, tomato pulp, and a sauce made of 1 tablespoon cornstarch, ½ cup mushroom water, 1 teaspoon sugar, 1 tablespoon soya sauce. Scramble and fry mixture 2 minutes. Serve.

揚 州 蝦 球

Yang Chow Haah Kow   Yang Chow Shrimp Balls

3 lbs. fresh shrimps (or prawns)	*1 cup flour*
¼ lb. pure fat pork	*1 tsp. salt*
4 egg whites	*vegetable oil*

Shell shrimps or prawns, wash thoroughly in water with salt and baking soda. Drain and mince to pulp. Mince-dice fat pork and chop roughly a little. In large mixing bowl cream the two ingredients together with the hand. Add four egg whites, ½ cup flour, and 1 tablespoon water in which is dissolved 1 teaspoon salt. Blend ingredients by stirring with the hand in one direction. After 15 to 20 minutes, pick up mass and toss back into bowl with vindictive vengefulness. In a while shrimps will turn white and lose their greyness. Continue stirring in one direction and tossing mass until quite stiff and of slightly pinkish tone. In about ½ hour mass should have acquired quite an adhering quality. Test by squeezing a little lump of shrimp mixture into bowl of cold water. If lump of shrimp mixture holds its shape well and does not begin to disintegrate or become sticky and shapeless when lightly touched by the fingers, it is ready for deep-fat frying.

Heat about ½ inch vegetable oil in skillet. Take mass of shrimp in your left hand. Squeeze generous lump of shrimp mixture through the hollow between thumb and base of index finger.

Shape delicately into as round a ball as possible and drop carefully into hot vegetable oil. Fry the walnut-sized lumps until puffed to almost three times their original size and a rich spun-gold hue on the outside. Serve. Makes about 30 balls.

豆 豉 龍 蝦

Dow See Loong Haah   Cantonese Lobster

1 live lobster (1½ lbs.)   1 tsp. salt
2 tbls. dow see (black fermented   ¼ tsp. pepper
    beans)   1 tsp. sugar
¼ lb. minced loin pork   1 tbls. cornstarch
1 clove garlic   2 cups broth
                          2 eggs

Kill lobster the spinal way. Chop off claws and legs. Then split lobster lengthwise and discard all undesirable parts like stomach and intestinal canal. When these have been removed, chop lobster meat in shell into manageable pieces. Chop legs and claws at joints and crack shells.

Mix minced pork with salt, pepper, sugar, ½ teaspoon cornstarch. crushed black fermented beans, and tablespoon vegetable oil. Heat a little oil in a pan, fry minced garlic and then add meat mixture. Fry a moment, then drop in pieces of lobster in shell. Fry another moment and then pour in hot broth to reach almost the level of the lobster. Simmer 10 minutes or until lobster is done.

Then mix remaining cornstarch with sufficient cold water and add slowly to simmering gravy. When gravy is thick, take pan off fire and stir in 2 beaten eggs. Pour into serving dish and serve right away.

Chapter VI

POULTRY

In China there are many superstitions and tales involving poultry. Even the coloring of the plumage of our feathered friends plays a great part in distinguishing them for varying omens and purposes in the field of superstition as well as in the world of culinary arts.

The cock is the incarnation of *Yeung* 陽 which represents all the warm and positive elements of universal life. Besides this, he also symbolizes five virtues. The crown upon his head indicates literary spirit; the spurs upon his feet mark a warlike disposition; his willingness to fight off his enemies displays his courage; his consideration for his mate by sharing grub and grain depicts his benevolence; and his punctuality in crowing to chase the ghosts away and to hail the coming of day symbolizes his faithfulness.

Ducks 鴨 *gnaap* in China are emblems of felicity. However, when ducks are found in pairs, they indicate conjugal fidelity.

Pairs of ducks, especially mandarin ducks, famed for their exquisite coloring, usually develop a strong attachment for their mates and will pine and die away if separated.

The pigeon 白 鴿 *baak gup,* although not believed to be the wisest of birds, is admired for its benevolence and its filial duty toward its mate and young. At the first sign of bad weather, the male is often seen sending his mate away to serener horizons, allowing her to return to nest only upon fair weather. In the caring of their young, the parent pigeons thoroughly macerate the food before feeding it to their tender offspring. Thus the dove and the pigeon are symbols of faithfulness, impartiality, longevity; and, especially, of filial duty.

The flesh of poultry is used in a great variety of forms in our diet. Besides being used freshly killed, it is often dried or salted and used as tasty tidbits or flavoring. The meat is not only appetizingly tender and fragrant, but also extremely rich in nutritious and beneficial values.

When purchasing poultry, the safest thing to do is to rely upon roasters and broilers. Choose a bird that is plump, has smooth, moist skin, and flexible, yielding breastbone, wings, legs, and feet. If a fatty bird is desired, choose one with yellowish moist skin; but, if tenderness only is in mind, choose one with satiny white skin.

When a recipe calls for fillet of chicken only, the easiest thing to do is to go to a poultry shop and purchase chicken breasts instead of a whole chicken 雞 *ghuy.* This will save the trouble of going through the tedium of boning a chicken.

Roasting chickens are young, usually anywhere from 5 to 9 months old and weigh from 3½ to 5½ pounds. Broilers weigh around 2 pounds, are extremely tender, but have one drawback in that they usually possess more weight in bone than meat. Roasting ducks run from 4 to 7 pounds. Before buying a duck, be sure that it is around 5 to 6 months old. To discover whether the duck will be tender or not, pinch the windpipe. If it is rubbery and elastically

111

supple, the duck will be tender; but if the windpipe is stiff to the pinch, resists, or cracks, then look for a younger bird.

燒 鴨

Sieu Ghuy   Barbecued Chicken

½ roasting chicken	½ tsp. heung new fun (spices
2 tbls. soya sauce	of five fragrances)
1 tsp. sugar	1 tbls. salad oil
1 clove garlic	1 pinch pepper
	½ tsp. salt

Mix all ingredients into sauce and rub thoroughly into chicken. After allowing sauce to soak in for about 10 minutes, place chicken on medium-hot grill or in medium hot oven. Roast or grill chicken 30 to 40 minutes. Baste and turn chicken at intervals to insure rich even browning. When chicken is cooked to succulent juicy tenderness, take cleaver and chop into fricassee pieces, or slice-chop in the Chinese manner, that is, chop little lengths about ¾ inch wide each.

陰 陽 鷄

Yum Yeung Ghuy   Light-shade Skewered Chicken

1 lb. fillet of chicken	½ tsp. sugar
¼ lb. sliced smoked ham	½ tsp. cornstarch
2 tsp. soya sauce	¼ tsp. salt
	1 pinch pepper

Cut chicken fillet into sheets as large as possible. Spread with a mixture of sugar, salt, pepper, cornstarch, and soya sauce. Place slice of ham to cover entire surface of slice of chicken, and fold the two layers over in half lengthwise. Roll folded piece of chicken and ham lengthwise around skewer, and tie securely with length of string. Place skewers in moderately heated oven or grill and cook 20 to 30 minutes. Turn and brush with oil after the first 10 minutes. The surface should be a rich golden brown tinted delicately with red. Untie string, draw out skewer, and slice length of chicken and ham diagonally into ½-inch segments.

紙 包 鷄

Jee Bow Ghuy	Paper-wrapped Chicken

½ lb. chicken fillet
¼ lb. sliced smoked ham
1 tbls. soya sauce
1 tbls. salad oil
1 tsp. cornstarch

½ tsp. salt
1 tsp. sugar
¼ tsp. pepper
3 dozen squares of tissue paper cut 4″ × 4″

1 tbls. sherry

Cut the fillet of chicken into pieces about ⅛ inch thick by ½ inch wide by 1½ inches long. Cut slices of ham into rectangles to match chicken surfaces. Mix chicken with sugar, pepper, salt, soya sauce, cornstarch, oil, and sherry. Place chicken slice on square of tissue paper, place slice of ham over it, and then gift-wrap package in the Chinese manner (see illustration). To Chinese gift-wrap the package, place chicken and ham in position No. 2. Fold over paper at dotted lines, and tuck in flap No. 6 so that package is securely closed.

Heat vegetable oil about 1 inch deep in frying pan and when sufficiently hot, carefully drop paper-wrapped chicken packages into oil. Fry packages from 1 to 1½ minutes on each side. The meat

113

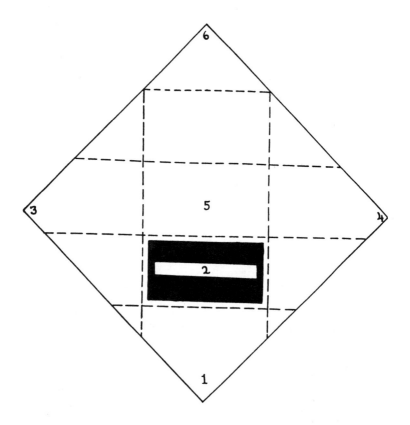

Chinese method of gift-wrapping paper-wrapped chicken

showing through the grease-soaked paper should be a rich golden speckled with sienna and red. Drain packages of oil and serve hot. Unwrap packages at the table. If desired, dip unwrapped contents into Worcestershire sauce to enhance the flavor.

114

碁于鷄

Kay Jee Ghuy   Chicken Chessmen

1 cup fillet of chicken	1 tbls. soya sauce
½ cup bamboo shoots	½ tsp. salt
4 slices smoked ham	¼ tsp. pepper
4 large Chinese mushrooms	1 tsp. sugar
1 length pig's intestine	1 tsp. cornstarch
1 tbls. sherry	1 tbls. oil

Dice chicken. Fine-dice bamboo shoots, slices of ham, and soaked mushrooms. Blend ingredients with sherry, soya sauce, pepper, salt, sugar, cornstarch, oil, and two tablespoons of water. Wash the pig's intestine thoroughly and soak in strong solution of salt, baking soda, and water. Be sure that the intestine is absolutely clean.

Use large funnel with neck about ¾ inch in diameter. Slip intestine up around neck of funnel and knot end of intestine securely. Hold funnel and intestine in place with one hand, and stuff ingredients into funnel with other hand. Gradually ingredients will fill intestine and form sausage about 4 feet long and about 1 to 1½ inches in diameter.

When all ingredients are in intestine, knot end securely. Prick surface of sausage with sharp-pronged fork in order to make holes through which steam may escape. Roast sausage in moderate oven about 20 minutes; turn sausage over and roast another 10 to 20 minutes, or until sausage is rich golden brown speckled with red. Cut sausage with razor-sharp knife into ½-inch-thick disks, called chessmen. Sprinkle lightly with Worcestershire sauce if desired.

磨菇炒鷄片

Maw Gwooh Chow Ghuy Pien—Mushroom Braised Velvet Chicken

1 *can white button mushrooms*	1 *tsp. salt*
3 *pairs chicken breasts*	1 *clove garlic (if desired)*
1 *slice ginger*	1 *tsp. soya sauce*
2 *tbls. vegetable oil*	1 *tbls. cornstarch*
¼ *tsp. white pepper*	¼ *cup mushroom water*

Slice chicken with shredlike thinness. Mix with 1 teaspoon cornstarch, ½ teaspoon salt, pepper, soya sauce, and vegetable oil. Heat mushrooms with sauce made of 2 teaspoons cornstarch and ½ teaspoon salt dissolved in ¼ cup of mushroom water. Chop ginger and garlic and fry in a little hot vegetable oil. Add chicken and fry over hot fire until semirare (about ½ minute). Pour in hot mushroom mixture and continue frying together until chicken turns white all over and is *just* done. Serve hot and quickly. Care must be taken not to overcook chicken.

滑鷄

Waaht Ghuy   Braised Satin Chicken

½ *roasting chicken*	½ *cup hot water*
1 *slice ginger minced*	1 *tbls. sherry*
4 *Chinese mushrooms*	1 *tbls. soya sauce*
12 gum jum *(golden needles)*	¼ *tsp. salt*
¼ *cup* wun yee *(cloud ears)*	¼ *tsp. pepper*
	½ *tsp. sugar*

Mix sugar, salt, pepper, ginger, soya sauce, and sherry together and rub well into chicken. Soak and clean mushrooms, cloud ears, and *gum jum*. Slice mushrooms, and cut *gum jum* in two. Heat a little oil in a casserole dish and brown chicken. Add soaked ingredients and ½ cup hot water. Bring contents to boil, cover casserole with lid, and turn down flame to allow contents to simmer until tender—about 30 to 40 minutes.

Place chicken on board and chop into neat slices about ¾-inch wide. Take out mushroom slices, *gum jum*, and *wun yee* and place in heap in serving dish. Arrange chicken neatly over them. Mix 1 tablespoon cornstarch with a little water, ¼ teaspoon sugar, and dash of soya sauce. Add to gravy of chicken. When reheated together and slightly thickened, pour sauce over chicken and serve immediately.

白斬鷄

Baak Jaahm Ghuy   White Cut Chicken

1 tender fat roasting or broiler chicken	*2 tbls. salt*
2 tbls. dry sherry (if desired)	*2 tbls. vegetable or Chinese sesame oil*

Submerge chicken in large pot of hot water to which salt and sherry have been added. Place the lid on pot, bring water to boil, and boil for 10 minutes. Turn off flame and allow chicken to cook in heat of water about 30 minutes. Take out chicken and rub with salad oil or sesame oil. Chop chicken with cleaver into neat seg-

ments about ¾-inch wide, and place neatly on dish. Serve with
sauce made of following ingredients:

1 large slice ginger minced
4 tbls. vegetable or sesame oil

1 tsp. salt
½ tsp. white pepper

青椒炒鷄片

Ching Jew Chow Ghuy Pien   Bell Pepper Braised Chicken

1 green bell pepper
1 red bell pepper
1 lb. chicken fillet
1 clove garlic
1 tbls. saang see jeung
6 scallions

4 stalks celery
1 tsp. soya sauce
1 tsp. cornstarch
1 tbls. vegetable oil
¼ tsp. pepper
½ tsp. salt

½ tsp. sugar

Slice chicken across grain into ¼-inch-thick 1-inch squares. Mix
with *saang see jeung*, oil, pepper, salt, sugar, and ½ teaspoon cornstarch. Mince garlic. Cut bell peppers into quarters, remove seeds
and membranes, and cut peppers into 1-inch squares. Chop scallions and celery stalks diagonally into ½-inch lengths.

Make sauce of ½ teaspoon cornstarch, soya sauce, pinch of sugar,
and a little water.

Heat a little oil in a skillet, fry celery and bell peppers with pinch
of salt about 1 minute. Cover skillet with lid and braise another
minute before adding scallions. Braise together, and after 1 to 2
minutes remove to dish. Fry garlic, add chicken, braise a moment,
stir ingredients, add bell peppers, and then pour in sauce. Fry a
moment until done and then serve immediately.

118

合桃鷄

Haap To Ghuy

Chicken Walnuts

½ lb. fillet of chicken
1 cup walnut meat (or unblanched
  fried pecans)
2 slices smoked ham
1 tbls. vegetable oil

½ tsp. cornstarch
1 tbls. soya sauce
¼ tsp. pepper
½ tsp. salt
¼ tsp. sugar

Slice fillet of chicken into thin sheets across the grain and cut
into 1-inch or so squares. Mix with cornstarch, 1 teaspoon soya
sauce, ¼ teaspoon each salt, pepper, sugar, and oil. Blanche walnuts and fry in hot oil until a golden hue. Drain nuts and salt
lightly with ¼ teaspoon salt. Heat a little oil in skillet and fry chick-
en a moment. Add ham, sliced into 1-inch squares, and walnuts.
Sprinkle with remaining soya sauce and fry until chicken is just
done.

喀喱鷄

Gaah Li Ghuy

Curried Chicken

1 4-lb. roasting chicken or
  2 2½-lb. fryers
4 tbls. curry powder
2 lb. onions
¼ lb. butter
2-3 tbls. vinegar

4 tbls. tomato paste
2 tbls. sugar
1 tsp. chile powder
1 tbls. salt
½ tsp. pepper
2 cloves garlic

Chop chicken into fricassee segments, sprinkle with salt and pepper and brown in hot oil. Make sauce by mixing curry powder
(more than given in recipe may be used), vinegar, tomato paste,
sugar, and chile powder (more or less than given in recipe may be
used). Slice onions thin and fry slowly in butter in deep casserole.

119

When onions are tender and juicy, add sauce, garlic, and chicken segments. Cover casserole with lid, turn down flame and allow contents to simmer slowly. After an hour, add salt and pepper to taste. Simmer another hour or until chicken is extremely tender. Stir at times during cooking to prevent sticking and burning. If much fat rises to the surface, skim all off carefully and keep for future use.

甜酸鷄肝

Tiem Shün Ghuy Gon   Sweet-Sour Chicken Livers

½ lb. chicken livers, hearts, and gizzards	2 slices ginger
½ cucumber	½ cup vinegar
2 stalks celery	3 tbls. sugar
1 carrot	1 tsp. salt
1 clove garlic	1 tsp. soya sauce
	1 tbls. cornstarch

Wash chicken livers, hearts, and gizzards. Split hearts and spread open. Cut gizzards into flowers by slitting almost through in horizontal slices $1/16$ inch apart and then cutting perpendicularly across first slits. Pour boiling water over liver, hearts, and gizzards and allow to soak 20 minutes.

In the meanwhile cut cucumber lengthwise, scrape out pulp and seeds, and cut cucumber into substantial diagonally sliced pieces. Slice celery and carrot diagonally. Rub cucumber, carrot, and celery with ½ teaspoon salt and allow to soak ten minutes. Pour the vinegar, 2 tablespoons sugar, and 2 tablespoons water over vegetables and allow to marinate at least 20 minutes.

Drain off vinegar from vegetables and make sauce by adding soya sauce, 1 tablespoon cornstarch, and 1 tablespoon sugar.

Heat a little oil in a pan, fry ginger and garlic a few moments and then add chicken livers, hearts, and gizzard flowers. Sprinkle with ½ teaspoon salt and a pinch of pepper. Stir, cover pot with lid, and braise 3 to 5 minutes. Add cornstarch mixture, stir until thickened, add vegetables, and braise 2 to 5 minutes or until chicken livers are done.

菠 蘿 鷄

Baw Law Ghuy   Pineapple Chicken

½ lb. fillet of chicken   1 tbls. cornstarch
1 small can pineapple   1 tbls. soya sauce
½ clove garlic   1 pinch pepper
1 tbls. salad oil   ½ tsp. salt

Parsley

Slice chicken and mix with 1 teaspoon cornstarch, pepper, oil, salt, and 1 teaspoon soya sauce. Cut pineapple slices into wedges. Heat a little oil in skillet and fry chicken until just underdone. Add pineapple. Cover skillet with lid and braise chicken and pineapple together 3 minutes. Remove to dish. Mix together 2 teaspoons soya sauce, 2 tablespoons water, 4 tablespoons pineapple water, and 2 teaspoons cornstarch. Heat a little oil and fry minced garlic, add sauce mixture and stir until thickened. Pour sauce over pineapple and chicken. Serve. Garnish dish with parsley.

風 栗 鷄

Foong Lüt Ghuy   Chicken Chestnuts

½ tender roasting chicken   2 tbls. dry sherry
1 lb. chestnuts   2 tbls. soya sauce
1 small piece ginger   1 tsp. sugar
3 scallions   1 tsp. salt
1 pint boiling water or broth   ¼ tsp. pepper

Chop chicken into fricassee segments. Slice ginger and smash each piece once. Use scallions whole, including leafy portion. Mix

121

chicken with sherry, soya sauce, sugar, pepper, and fry in very little heated oil until golden brown. Add ginger, scallions, salt, and 1 pint water or broth or stock. Cover pot with lid and allow chicken to simmer 40 to 60 minutes or until tender.

In the meanwhile, shell and blanche chestnuts. Boil for 15 minutes, then cut in half. Add chestnuts to chicken and simmer together for another 15 minutes or until chicken is tender.

炸 白 鴿

Jaah Baak Gup   Browned Squab

2 *squabs*	¼ *tsp. salt*
1 *tsp. soya sauce*	1 *pinch pepper*
Vegetable oil	

Split squabs along spines and spread open. Rub with salt, pepper, and soya sauce. Heat vegetable oil for deep-fat frying and when oil is sufficiently hot, fry squab for 15 minutes. Squab should be cooked to juicy succulence and should have a rich reddish brown hue. Drain squab and serve in halves or chopped in neat slices ½-to ¾-inch wide. Serve with lime or lemon slices.

清蒸白鴿

Ching Jing Baak Gup   Steamed Velvet Squab

1 *fat tender squab*	1 *tsp. soya sauce*
1 *slice smoked ham*	½ *tsp. cornstarch*
12 *golden needles* (gum jum)	½ *tsp. salt*
2 *Chinese mushrooms*	½ *tsp. sugar*
2 *scallions*	1 *pinch pepper*
2 *Chinese red dates* (hoong joe)	1 *tbls. vegetable oil*
1 *slice ginger*	

Chop squab into small pieces and mix with soya sauce, corn-starch, salt, sugar, pepper, and oil. Soak *gum jum,* mushrooms, and red dates, slice, and add to squab. Chop ginger and scallions and mix with squab. Cut ham into matchlike strips and use as garnish over squab. Place dish of squab in steamer and steam about 35 to 40 minutes or until done.

磨菇炆白鴿

Maw Gwooh Mun Baak Gup   Casserole of Mushroom Squabs

4 tender fat squabs	16 fresh white mushrooms or 1 small
2 tbls. soya sauce	can button mushrooms
2 slices smoked ham	1 tsp. sugar
1 tbls. dry sherry	½ tsp. salt
1 slice ginger	¼ lb. sugar peas (mange tout)
½ tsp. heung new fun spices	2 tsp. cornstarch

Split squabs along spines and spread out flat. Rub well with soya sauce, allowing 1 teaspoon soya sauce for each squab. Heat a little oil in a pan and fry squabs skin side down to rich brown hue. Place the squabs in casserole, skin side up, and spread in between with slices of ham. Sprinkle squab with salt, sugar, *heung new fun* (powdered spices of five fragrances), 2 teaspoons soya sauce, and sherry. Pour boiling water over squabs until water level equals that of squabs. Cover pot with lid and allow contents to simmer slowly for 1 hour. Add mushrooms and continue to sim-mer squabs about 1 hour or so more until tender.

In the meanwhile braise sugar peas in small amount of boiling water and pinch of soda, 1 teaspoon vegetable oil, and 1 teaspoon salt. Drain and use for garnish.

To serve, place squab carefully on attractive platter. Garnish all around with green sugar peas, mushrooms, and ham. Reheat sauce and thicken with 2 teaspoons cornstarch dissolved in a little water. When thickened, pour over squabs. Serve.

HOW TO BONE A DUCK

Take a fat undressed duck. Chop off lower wings and legs. Then using sharp knife or cleaver, cut skin carefully along spine. Working close to the bone, remove the scanty flesh, separating it carefully so as not to tear either flesh or skin. When thigh joint is reached, lift leg and work it around in all directions in order to loosen joint; then insert corner point of blade of cleaver and hit cleaver lightly but firmly until joint separates from pelvis. In the case of the shoulder, work around bone until the supple joint and socket is reached. Insert point of blade of cleaver and cut joint and socket apart.

When fleshier portion of duck is reached, alternately cut and tear flesh away from bones. When bone case is cleanly loose of all flesh, draw out bony neck through skin as far as possible, and chop off. Then draw out windpipe and esophagus. Cut off tail bone and lower intestine as far as possible within tail, but do not chop off tail. Remove oil sacks carefully. Wash duck in cold water and hang up by tail to drain thoroughly. Use bones, lower wings, legs and neck for broth.

Gaah Heung Ngaap   Home-Style Duck

1 *tender fat duck*	2 *tsp. sugar*
1 *medium-sized piece ginger*	3 *tsp. soya sauce*
2 *Spanish onions*	2 *tsp. salt*
½ *cup* cho-gwooh *(dried sliced Italian mushrooms make a good substitute)*	1 *tbls. sherry*
	¼ *tsp. pepper*
	½ *tsp.* heung new fun *spices*
1 *clove garlic*	1 *lb. fresh spinach*

Bone duck, wash, and hang by base of neck to drain thoroughly. Then spread duck out, and draw semiboned neck up and lay along center of duck so that the tip of the neck is toward the tail. Spread on duck filling made according to following recipe: Slice 2 Spanish onions and fry until golden. Mince garlic and ginger. Soak and clean *cho-gwooh* or dried mushroom slices. Add sugar, 2 teaspoons soya sauce, salt, sherry, pepper, and *heung new fun*. Sew duck together securely.

Place about 1 cup boiling water in bowl which contained filling and use liquid as sauce. Heat about $1/16$ inch of oil in pot. Rub duck with 1 teaspoon soya sauce, and lay duck unsewn side down in heated oil to brown. When thoroughly browned, turn duck over in pot, pour sauce over it, and then add enough boiling water to barely cover duck. Cover pot with lid, and simmer contents slowly at least 4 hours or until the duck is extremely puffed and tender.

To serve, braise fresh spinach with ½ cup sauce from cooking duck. Lay spinach in ring on serving dish, and place duck, sewed side under, on spinach. Garnish with parsely or scallion-carrot ring flowers if desired.

京醬鴨

Ging Jeung Ngaap   Peking* Sauce Duck

1 *tender fat duck*	3 *tbls.* hoy sien jeung *sauce*
2 *Spanish onions*	1 *tsp. sugar*
1 *clove garlic*	¼ *tsp. salt*
1 *slice ginger*	¼ *tsp. pepper*
3 *tsp. soya sauce*	½ *tsp.* heung new fun *spices*
1 *tbls. sherry*	1 *lb. fresh spinach*

* Since the capital of China moved south to *Nanking* in 1911, the city of *Peking* 北京 (northern capital) has since changed its name to *Peiping* 北平 (northern peace).

Bone duck, wash, and hang by base of neck to drain thoroughly. Then spread duck out, skin side down, and draw semiboned neck up and lay along center of duck so that the tip of the neck is toward the tail. Spread on duck filling made according to following recipe: Slice 2 Spanish onions into coarse wedges and fry until golden. Mince garlic and ginger. Mix together, fried onions, garlic, ginger, *hoy sien jeung* (sauce), 2 teaspoons soya sauce, sherry, sugar, salt, pepper, and *heung new fun* spices. Then sew duck securely together. Pour 1 cup boiling water into bowl which contained stuffing and use resulting liquid as weak sauce.

Heat a little oil in a large pot, rub duck with 1 teaspoon soya sauce, and lay duck unsewed side down in hot oil to brown. When thoroughly browned, turn duck over, pour weak sauce over it, and then add enough boiling water to barely cover duck. Cover pot with lid and allow contents to simmer slowly about 4 hours or until duck is extremely puffed and tender.

To serve, braise 1 pound fresh spinach with ½ cup gravy from duck. Add salt to taste if necessary. Spread spinach in ring on platter and lay duck, unsewed side up, on spinach. Garnish duck with parsley or with scallion-carrot ring flower if desired.

Three-In-One Duck

Three delicious duck dishes may be obtained from one duck as a result of one roasting. They are *Sieu Ngaap* 烧鸭 Roast Duck, *Baw Law Ngaap* 波萝鸭 Pineapple Duck, and *Sieu Ngaap Jook* 烧鸭粥 Roast Duck Congee (see under *Rice and Mien Dishes*). This economical trio of dishes allows for absolutely no wastage. The boneless breast meat is used for Pineapple Duck; the thigh or drumstick, shoulder or upper wing, and the meat and bone from the back areas are chopped into neat slices about ½ to ¾ inch wide, arranged upon a dish, and served as pure Roast Duck; and the lower legs, lower wings, neck, and remaining bones are used to make congee. The recipes of the first two dishes are given in the following pages, but the recipe for Roast Duck Congee is given in the chapter on Rice and Mien Dishes (see page 165).

Sieu Ngaap   Roast Duck

1 tender fat duck complete with neck and head	½ tsp. pepper
1 clove garlic	1 tsp. sugar
4 tsp. saang see jeung (sauce)	1 tsp. salt
½ tsp. heung new fun spice	1 tbls. soya sauce
1 tsp. honey	2 tbls. sherry

Make a sauce by mixing crushed garlic, *saang see jeung* (aromatic sauce), *heung new fun,* pepper, sugar, salt, soya sauce, and sherry. Pour sauce into duck and rub thoroughly all over inner surface. Sew up opening and wipe entire outer surface of duck clean. Gripping duck by neck over the hole in its neck, blow air into space between skin and bony neck portion until duck becomes puffed to the limit. Grip neck below hole immediately so that air will not escape and then tie string around neck securely (see illustration, page 128).

Dissolve honey in 1 cup boiling water. Hold duck by neck over basin and pour honeyed water over duck about eight times. In the meanwhile, have oven heated moderately hot and place duck in it upon shallow roasting pan breast side up about 3 to 4 inches from heat. When entire top surface of duck turns to a smooth rich reddish brown—after 15 to 20 minutes—turn duck over, and roast about 20 minutes. Brush surface with drippings at times during roasting. Turn off heat and allow to roast in heat of oven about

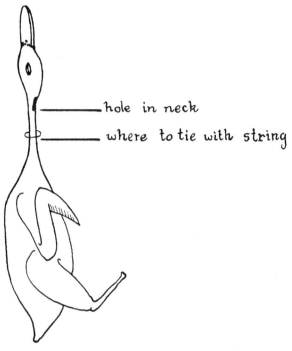

hole in neck

where to tie with string

How to prepare a blown duck for roasting

10 to 15 minutes. Place duck on rack to drain and cool. Pour all drippings into bowl to use as sauce for Roast Duck.

When duck is cool, cut open threads and pour sauce into bowl containing drippings. Split duck along spine into two portions. Remove legs at thigh joints, and remove wings at shoulder joints. Carefully tear off breast meat. Use breast meat and thigh meat for Pineapple Duck. Use neck, head, bones, lower wings and legs for Roast Duck Congee. Use drumstick, wings, and back area of duck for Roast Duck. Chop these portions into neat slices about ½-to ¾-inch wide, arrange slices on platter, pour sauce from roast duck over and serve.

128

菠蘿鴨

Baw Law Ngaap   Pineapple Duck

1 pair breast meat and thigh meat from roast duck	1 tsp. salt
½ fresh pineapple	¼ cup snow-white sesame seeds
½ Spanish onion	¼ cup white vinegar
1 small piece young ginger	1 tbls. English mustard
	2 tsp. sugar
1 tbls. salad oil	

Shred onion and ginger into fine shreds. Rub with ½ teaspoon salt and allow to marinate 10 minutes. Add a mixture of 1½ teaspoons sugar, 3 tablespoons vinegar, and allow onion and ginger to marinate ½ hour more.

Toast sesame seeds in small frying pan over extremely low fire. Stir constantly. If heat becomes too great and seeds start popping, remove pan from fire temporarily. Toast seeds to light golden hue, spread out on saucer, and when cool crush gently with rolling pin.

Mix English mustard, 1 tablespoon vinegar, and ½ teaspoon sugar with 1 tablespoon water. Stir and stir until mustard actually begins to smell hot. Cover and place in warm spot until needed.

Cut fillet of roast duck into ⅛-inch-thick slices. Add ¼ teaspoon salt, mustard mixture, and crushed sesame seeds. Drain ginger and onions and add to duck mixture. Sprinkle with 1 tablespoon salad oil. Add pineapple slices, mix together thoroughly, and serve.

HOW TO PREPARE FRESH PINEAPPLE

Cut off top and base of pineapple. Stand pineapple on end and using sharp knife cut skin off in strips with firm down motion. Cut diagonal wedged ruts down the paths of little black cores. Quarter pineapple lengthwise, remove woody heart from each piece, and then slice pineapple into ¼-inch-thick pieces. Mix pieces of pineapple with duck mixture.

Chapter VII

PURE MEAT DISHES

Methods of hunting and trapping
(*Pictographs of the Yin Period* (1400 B. C.)

MEAT in early periods of Chinese history was eaten in far greater quantities than today. Anthropologists record that the prehistoric "Peking Man" (500,000 to 100,000 years ago), who dwelt in tree nests and mountain caves, used crude implements and methods for hunting down his prey. They clothed themselves in the furs and hides of the animals and ate of the flesh. It is supposed that they ate their meat raw, although recent excavations have found that the Peking Man had in his time already mastered the art of producing fire. Heaps of charcoal ashes and animal bones bearing the traces of having been burned have been excavated, but no proofs were found as to the true state of the meat or food when eaten. By 40,000 B. C., however, the people had learned the finer arts of hunting, fishing, and the cruder methods of cooking.

130

Yin Period (1400 B. C.) pictographs inscribed upon bones and shells relate the historical methods used in hunting and trapping prior to and during the Shang Dynasty (1523-1027 B. C.).

Today, most peoples in China eat domesticated animals only namely: pork, beef, and mutton.

Ngow 牛 oxen in China are great friends and helpers of the peasant. Their faithful services, great strength, and constant patience are so valued and appreciated that they are rarely relished as food.

Ceremonial plowing ... Beating of the "Spring Ox"

131

Around the fifth of February, there is a farmer's festival called "The Meeting of the Spring" 迎 春 *Yieng chün.* Since the ox is the emblem of "spring" and "agriculture," he takes part in these festivities of ceremonial ploughing and beating of the "Spring Ox" 春 牛 *Chün Ngow.* The Spring Ox is made of clay and is beaten with sticks to promote and encourage the coming of spring. Each year, according to accurate astronomical and geomantic calculations and omens, the details of the ox and driver are carefully worked out. It is said that if the ox is yellow, the peasants may expect a fruitful year and an extraordinarily abundant harvest. If the ox is red, there will be painful tragedy and fire; and if the ox is white, there will be death and mourning. The approach of an ordinary spring can be predicted when the cowherd is properly clad in all aspects; but, if the tail of the bull is uplifted, and the driver is stripped of his jacket or wears his trouser legs rolled up, it is an omen of an early spring. When the ox or just his tail is lying down, or the driver is properly shod, then it signifies that spring will take its time.

Yeung 羊 sheep, besides being the symbol for retired life, are also the emblem of filial piety. This is due to the fact that the lamb kneels respectfully by its mother as it takes her milk. Sheep are frequently used for sacrifice. Most Chinese do not care for the strong odor of mutton, but, since the meat is of excellent texture, it is a favorite food of the Chinese Mohammedan, who believes pork to be too unclean to be consumed by human beings.

Jü 猪 pigs, being lazy creatures that spend their days eating and sleeping, are the favorite meat-producing animals consumed by the Chinese. Killing and eating a loafing porker inflicts no pangs of conscience upon the eater; and, besides, the flesh is extremely tasty and fragrant.

In China, the word for home is 家 *gaah.* The Chinese character is written up as a combination of a roof 宀 over a pig 豕. This combination is probably derived from the fact that many Chinese villagers shelter their pigs under their roofs. In China as well as in many a European country, a pig or pigs in a home are a token of prosperity and plenty. Everyone knows the famous essay by Charles Lamb on the subject of pigs sheltered in homes and how the delights of roast pig were discovered in the dawn of Chinese history when a peasant's house burned down.

As a matter of fact, the Chinese have been known to cook their food since 40,000 B. C., a time around which fire is thought to have been discovered. According to tradition, a man by the name of *Sui Jen* learned the secret through watching a few woodpeckers hard at work hammering against the bark of a tree. He noticed sparks issuing forth as a result of the friction of the insistant bill against the wood. He devised a similar method of starting combustion by boring one stick into another. With the invention of fire, the people of China then proceeded to learn improved methods of domesticating animals, catching fish, and cooking food under the guidance of *Fook Hey.*

The earliest manner of cooking food was through a method of heating slabs of stone and then roasting the raw ingredients upon them. By the Shang Period (1523-1027 B.C.) cooking had become more developed, but it reached its fancy primitive heights around the early and middle Chow Dynasty (1027-474 B.C.). Recipes of that period were recorded upon bamboo slips, wooden panels, and sheets of silk. There is a recipe of that age which I pass on to you, admitting, with all frankness, that I have not attempted to test it. It is interesting to note, however, that cooking methods of today retain many of the ancient procedures found in this venerable father of recipes.

Take a suckling pig, clean inside and out, and replace its entrails with stuffing of sweet dates. Wrap in jacket of straw and reeds made adhering with fresh clay, and then bake in heated pit dug in ground. As soon as clay is dry it is broken off. Then crackling is removed by freshly washed hands and ground with rice flour until mixture has consistency of gruel. This is then mixed with cooked date stuffing, and fried in a quantity of hot lard sufficient to cover it. Next, place small pot supported by tripod within larger pot. Fill smaller pot with slices of pork and fragrant herbs and spices, and fill space between two pots with an amount of water which will not boil over into smaller pot. Attention must be given to the fire so that it will burn three days and three nights without stopping. After this, the remaining roast is served accompanied with additions of pickled pork and a mixture of fried crackling and dates.

烧 猪

Sieu Jüh   Roast Pig

> 2 lbs. pork with skin, and spare-ribs   ½ tsp. sugar
>   from loin area   1 tsp. honey
> 1 tsp. heung new fun spices   ¼ cup water
>   2 tsp. salt

Mix salt, sugar, and *heung new fun* together and rub the mixture into the meat surface of the pork. Prick the meat surface to enable the salt mixture to soak in deeply for about an hour. Then roast the pork in a moderately hot oven, meaty side up, and skin side down submerged in ½ cup water. Roast pork ½ hour, turn skin side up, prick skin surface thoroughly, and rub honey diluted in ¼ cup hot water into skin surface. Roast pork in moderate oven about 1 to 1½ hours more. Skin surface should be a rich reddish brown hue and crisply crackling. Remove bones carefully and cut pork into pieces with about ½″ x ½″ of skin surface to each piece of pork.

Yuen Taai   Round Ham of Pork

2 lbs. lower ham with skin   1 tbls. sugar
¼ cup soya sauce   1 tsp. salt
3 tbls. naam yü (sauce)   2 cloves garlic
¼ cup sherry   2 scallions

Clean, dehair, and scrape surface of skin of lower pork ham. Cut open ham lengthwise and carefully remove thighbone. Rub pork all over with 2 tablespoons soya sauce, and then brown skin side down in a little heated oil. Turn pork over, add garlic cloves, scallions, 1 teaspoon salt, a sauce made of naam yü, sherry, sugar, 2 tablespoons soya sauce, and ½ cup hot water. Fry ½ minute, and then add enough boiling water to cover at least an inch over surface of pork. Cover pot with lid and allow contents to simmer gently at least 4 hours or until pork is extremely tender.

A spinach base or a faat choy 髮菜 (hair vegetable) base may be served with the rich succulent pork. If spinach is used, braise 1 pound fresh spinach with ½ cup gravy from pork. When cooked but yet fresh and green, arrange spinach in ring on attractive platter. Place pork, skin side up, neatly upon it.

If faat choy is used, take ½ cup of the dried, hairlike seaweed and soak in hot water for 1 hour. Squeeze fresh water through until water comes out clear. Put seaweed in collander and pour 2 teaspoons oil over it. Squeeze oil into seaweed thoroughly, then squeeze more fresh water through it until it comes out clear. Drain the seaweed and pour 1 tablespoon cooking sherry over it. Squeeze in sherry thoroughly. After a few moments, rinse seaweed again with fresh water. Drain, and when vegetable is clear, shining, and clean, add to cooking pork ½ an hour before serving time.

135

As with the spinach, arrange *faat choy* on attractive platter, and then place the pork, skin side up, upon it.

义 烧

Chaah Sieu   Barbecued Pork

1 lb. lean loin pork	½ tsp. heung new fun *spices*
½ tsp. salt	1 tsp. sugar
¼ tsp. pepper	1 tsp. sherry

2 tbls. soya sauce

Cut lean pork along the grain into strips about 2 inches wide. Mix salt, pepper, sugar, and *heung new fun,* and rub mixture into pork. Allow the spicy flavor to soak in for a couple of hours. Heat oven to moderate. Rub sherry and soya sauce into pork and roast pork 10 minutes. Turn pork over, raise heat to high, baste meat with dripping, and roast pork another 15 minutes. Slice each strip against grain into ¼-inch-thick pieces.

紅 烧 猪 肉

Hoong Sieu Jüh Yook   Casserole of Five-Flowered Pork

2 lbs. ngung faah yook (five-flowered pork)	1 pint soya sauce
	4-5 cloves baat gok (Chinese anise)
¼ cup sherry	2 lbs. fresh spinach
1 leek	½ tsp. salt
1 bunch scallions	2 tbls. sugar
1 large piece ginger	

1 clove garlic

136

With a sharp knife, indicate 1-inch squares upon skin surface of pork. Then using cleaver, cut along those indicated lines through the pork to form pieces of five-flowered pork. Place these segments in bowl of cold water and about 2 tablespoons salt. Allow to soak 15 minutes, drain well, and then place in dry bowl. Sprinkle with sherry and allow to soak until time to use.

Cut leek and scallions into 3-inch lengths. Slice ginger and smash each slice with flat of blade of cleaver. Heat a little oil in a pot, fry leek, scallions, and ginger; then add pork and continue frying until pork is spotted with crusts of golden hue. Pour in enough soya sauce to reach two thirds the height of the pork, and then add enough boiling water to cover pork. Add sherry in which pork has soaked, sugar, garlic, and Chinese star anise. Bring mixture to boil, cover pot with lid, and allow contents to simmer gently for 1 hour. Skim off all surface fat and put in bowl. This surface fat is excellent for frying vegetables. Continue simmering another hour, skimming off surface fat at intervals. When fatty tissue of pork is translucent and tender, casserole of five-flowered pork is done. (Total cooking time 2 to 2½ hours.)

Now braise 2 pounds fresh spinach with about ½ cup or so of gravy from pork. Add salt to taste if necessary. When spinach is done but yet fresh and green, arrange on attractive platter. Drain pork cubes of sauce and arrange neatly upon spinach. Serve.

Allow gravy to cool and then remove island of surface fat to another dish. Strain sauce and pour into a jar. Place this in refrigerator and use as fragrant substitute for soya sauce.

烧 排 骨

Sieu Pi Gwut   Barbecued Spareribs

2 lbs. pork spareribs   2 tbls. naam yü *sauce*
½ tsp. heung new fun *spices*   2 tbls. *soya sauce*
1 tsp. salt   ½ tsp. *sugar*
                    ½ *clove garlic*

Place pork spareribs on a baking sheet. Using sharp knife, slice meat between bones once but almost through the thickness. Make sauce by crushing and blending garlic with *naam yü*, sugar, salt, soya sauce, and *heung new fun*. Rub sauce well into both surfaces and cracks of meat.

Bake spareribs in hot oven for 20 minutes on each side. Allow meat to attain rich reddish-brown color. When done, divide spareribs with knife. Serve hot. English mustard is an excellent accompaniment for Barbecued Spareribs.

甜 酸 排 骨

Tiem Shün Pi Gwut   Sweet-Sour Spareribs

1 lb. pork spareribs   ¼ tsp. chile powder
2 cloves garlic smashed   1½ tsp. salt
2 tbls. soya sauce   1 egg
½ cup vinegar   ½ cucumber
¼ cup heung new fun *spices*   1 carrot
¼ tsp. pepper   6 tbls. cornstarch
                    2 tbls. sugar

Slice spareribs through between bones, and then chop each sparerib into 1-inch pieces. Plunge into pot of boiling water, and

138

allow to stand for 15 minutes. Drain pieces of sparerib and then mix them with 1 tablespoon vinegar, 1 tablespoon soya sauce, ¼ teaspoon pepper, *heung new fun*, 1 teaspoon salt, 1 clove crushed garlic, 1 egg, and 5 tablespoons cornstarch. Stir until spareribs are coated with batter. Heat about 2 inches of vegetable oil in pot. Drop in spareribs and cook until done (10 to 15 minutes) and the batter acquires rich golden brown.

In the meanwhile, cut cucumber lengthwise, remove pulp and seeds, and diagonal-slice firmer portion. Slice carrot thin. Rub cucumber and carrot slices with ½ teaspoon salt and then add remainder of vinegar, chile powder, and 1 tablespoon sugar. Let vegetables marinate for at least 15 minutes.

After this time, drain vegetables and place in serving dish. Add 1 tablespoon sugar to vinegar, then mix with ¼ cup water, 1 tablespoon cornstarch, and 1 tablespoon soya sauce. Heat a little oil in a frying pan, fry garlic a few seconds, then stir in vinegar-cornstarch mixture. Cook until thickened. Toss in spareribs, and cook the two together about a minute. Arrange spareribs and sauce over marinated vegetables and serve.

甜酸猪脚

Tiem Shün Jüh Gerk   Sweet-Sour Pig's Feet
(Number 1)

4 *pig's feet*	1 *tbls. soya sauce*
1 *cup vinegar*	2 *thick slices ginger*
¼ *cup sugar*	¼ *tsp. chile powder*
¼ *cup* saang see jeung	½ *tsp. salt*
(*aromatic sauce*)	1 *clove garlic*

Clean pig's feet thoroughly and place in pot of cold water with about 2 tablespoons salt. Bring water to boil and allow pig's feet

139

to simmer for 5 minutes. Drain pig's feet and throw out salt water. Take cleaver and divide each foot into 5 or 6 pieces. Heat a little oil and fry ginger, then add pig's feet, and fry until they acquire a golden crust in spots. In the meanwhile, mix *saang see jeung*, sugar, soya sauce, crushed garlic, salt, and ¼ cup hot water. Add to frying pig's feet, cover pot with lid, and braise contents a few minutes. Then add vinegar and enough boiling water to barely cover pig's feet. Cover pot with lid, and simmer contents gently about 3 hours or until the pig's feet are extremely tender.

Sweet-Sour Pig's Feet

(Number 2)

6 *pig's feet*	4 *peppercorns*
3 *cups vinegar*	3 *cloves garlic*
1 *cup sugar*	3 *tbls. soya sauce*
1 *whole ginger root*	*Vegetable oil*
Salt and pepper	

Clean pig's feet and chop each into six to eight pieces. Place in enough hot water to cover and 2 tablespoons salt and bring to boil for 5 minutes. Drain, and scrape skin surface lightly to insure cleanliness. Heat ¼ inch of oil in pan. Rub pig's feet surface with soya sauce, salt and pepper lightly, and then tan in hot oil until a rich golden brown.

Boil vinegar, sugar, peeled ginger sliced paper thin, peppercorns, and cloves of garlic. Add pig's feet, soya sauce, enough water to barely cover (½ to 1 cup), and 2 tablespoons oil. Bring contents of pot to rapid boil, cover pot with lid, turn down flame, and simmer contents gently about 3 hours. Pig's feet should be tender but chewy, and of a rich mahogany hue. Liquid should have been reduced to savorsome sauce thick and gelatinous. Serve piping hot.

This dish may be reheated, but a little hot water must be added to prevent sticking and burning.

揚 州 獅 子 頭

Yang Chow See Jee Tao   Yang Chow Lion's Head

See jee tao 獅子頭 lions' heads are a specialty from *Yang Chow* (pronounced *Yeung Jow* in Cantonese). The lions' heads are peach-sized meat balls steamed or simmered gently with hearts of Chinese cabbage, which are supposed to resemble lions' manes. There is a superstition of the *Yang Chow Daai See Foohs* concerning this dish. They claim that when in molding the meat into balls the balls come out accidentally in even numbers, the dish will turn out very successfully and you will have good luck.

2 lbs. tenderloin of pork	¾ cup soya sauce
1 lb. pure fat pork	12 large Chinese mushrooms
¾ cup fresh crab meat	1 cup bamboo shoot
1 egg	12 hearts of Chinese cabbage
1 scallion	5 tsp. sugar
1 small piece ginger	1 tsp. salt

Bone tenderloin of pork and use bones for making broth. Simmer bones with 1 quart boiling water, ½ cup soya sauce, and 3 teaspoons sugar; remove bones to another dish after ½ hour; remove lid of pot, and turn off fire.

Shred crab meat and fry in very little oil and ½ teaspoon salt. Mince-dice lean pork, and then chop about eight times with cleaver. Fine-dice fat pork and then chop mass roughly about four times. Mince ginger and scallion. Put lean meat, fat pork, crab meat, ginger, scallion into large mixing bowl. Blend ingredients, stirring in one direction with pair of chopsticks or wooden spoon.

141

Do not use your hands or any metal implements. Add 2 teaspoons sugar, ½ teaspoon salt, and 1 egg. Stir thoroughly.

Have dish containing ¼ cup soya sauce in readiness. Moisten hands with cold water, grasp a mass of meat mixture with your fingers and delicately mold into peach-sized ball with palms of your hands. Dip ball into soya sauce and pat sauce all over surface of ball. Then gently, very gently, place ball in warm broth. Turn heat under broth to low heat (very lowest possible). If fire is too hot, balls of meat will contract too rapidly, fall apart, and possess a toughish, rough, dry texture.

When balls (about sixteen) are set, cover pot with lid, and raise fire to low heat. Do not dare to touch meat balls or move them or disturb broth around them during the first 15 minutes or before they become set and acquire a grayish hue. When broth begins to simmer very gently, turn down heat to the very lowest again, replace bones in pot, and then place lid on pot.

Soak mushrooms and add to meat balls after 1 hour of gentlest cooking. Continue to simmer in that manner for 3½ hours, and then add diced bamboo shoots and hearts of white cabbage. Simmer ½ hour more and serve.

If Chinese cabbage cannot be obtained, 2 pounds lima beans (fresh) will make a good substitute. Shell and husk lima beans and plunge into pot of boiling water containing pinch of soda. Simmer about 5 minutes and then drain. Add to meat balls ½ hour before they are finished cooking. Clusters of fresh spinach leaves and stems make a good substitute too, but care must be taken not to overcook the spinach. Add spinach not sooner than 10 or 15 minutes before meat balls are ready to be served.

紮 蹄

Jaak Taai   Bound Trotters

2 *tender young pig's feet with*	1 *tsp. sugar*
about four inches of ankle	¼ *cup soya sauce*
1 *lb. semifat loin of pork*	1 *clove garlic*
1 *tsp.* heung new fun *spices*	1 *tbls. salt*
8 *cloves* baat gok, *Chinese anise*	1 *tbls. sherry*
1 *large piece ginger*	

Clean pig's feet and ankle, plunge into pot of cold water and about 2 tablespoons salt. Bring water to boil, drain pig's feet and throw out salt water. Cut once along length of pig's feet and ankle, and remove all larger bones. Cut loin pork into thin strips about 4 inches long and soak in sauce made of sherry, 1 tablespoon soya sauce, sugar, 1 teaspoon salt, and ½ teaspoon *heung new fun.* Spread open pig's feet and fill with strips of soaked meat. Sew up stuffed pig's feet, or bind pig's feet securely together with a length of string.

Make a sauce by boiling garlic, ginger, ½ tsp. *heung new fun, baat gok* (Chinese star anise), and 2 teaspoons salt in 1 quart boiling water for 15 minutes. Add bound pig's trotters, 3 tablespoons soya sauce, and enough boiling water to cover trotters. Cover pot with lid, bring contents to boil, turn down fire, and allow contents to simmer gently for 4 to 5 hours or until bound trotters are very, very tender.

Unbind trotters and serve. Keep sauce for future use. It would be much more attractive if one served the piglet looking trotters on a layer of braised fresh spinach. Braise about 1 pound fresh spinach with ½ cup gravy from pork, and when cooked but yet crisp and freshly green, arrange on attractive platter, then place piglet trotters decoratively on bed of spinach and serve.

喫喱牛腩

Gaah Li Ngow Naam

Curried Beef Plate

2 lbs. 100 abdomen of beef (muscular plate area) ngow baak naam
1 large firm ripe tomato
1 Spanish onion

2 cloves garlic
¼ cup curry powder
1 tsp. chile powder
2 tsp. salt
1 tbls. sugar

Place beef in large pot of cold water and bring water to boil. Drain meat and throw out water. Wash beef and cut into 1-inch cubes. Dice tomato, slice onion, and mince garlic. Heat a little oil in a casserole dish, fry onions, and when they are juicily tender, stir in curry powder. Add tomato and garlic. Fry a moment and add cubes of beef, sugar, and salt. Fry another 5 minutes and then add enough boiling water to barely cover beef. Bring water to boil, cover pot with lid, turn down fire, and allow contents to simmer gently about 3 hours or until beef is extremely tender and muscular areas are gelatinous. Potatoes may be added, but fry in deep fat until they acquire a golden crust before you add them to curry. Frying enhances flavor of the potatoes.

Chapter VIII

VEGETABLE DISHES

The Chinese word *"fooh"* 富 signifies abundance, prosperity, and enrichment. It exemplifies the embodiment of man's hope to exist in peace and plenty, and so the word is written up as: a roof ⼧ symbolizing shelter and security; one ⼝ mouth 口 indicating unity and understanding; and a field 田, expressing man's ability to reap rewards of richness and plenty through diligence and faithful toiling.

Agriculture is the major occupation of the Chinese people today and has been ever since time immemorial. The pictographs of the Yin Period (1400 B. C.) indicate cultivation of the soil as the main occupation of man by representing the word "male" as a written combination of a plow upon a field 男 (see illustration, page 146). Later the plow was modified for the word strength 力.

Shen Nung (2737 B. C.), whose name means "Divine Husband-man," is regarded as the father of the art of tilling the soil and the inventor of improved farming implements. His curiosity regarding plant life, and his willingness to use his own stomach and body as a laboratory resulted in the discovery of a wider assortment of vegetables and herbs for eating and medicinal purposes. Much later, during the Yin Period, a new system of land division occurred. Land was alotted to groups of eight families, each receiving sixteen

Yin Period pictograph representing the word "male"

acres. In the center, there was a ninth field of equal size belonging to the landowner or the state. A well was placed in this plot of ground, and four paths led from it to the other lands. As a result the word denoting "well" is derived from this type of land separation. All eight families shared in the tilling of the central plot, and the money received from the selling of the harvest went into the paying of the land taxes of all the fields.

The great variety of climate and soil resulting from China's size has favored the cultivation of an enormous diversity of plants. The abundant vegetation allows for economizing on the eating of flesh. But, in spite of the sparing use of meat, the Chinese have developed a fairly well-balanced diet. This is through instinct and long experience rather than through science. The bean curd, for example, offers sufficient proteins, vegetable oils, roughage, vitamins, and salts. Also, Chinese cooking in itself retains the freshness, greenness, and all the beneficial elements of the vegetables.

When peoples abroad think of agriculture and the raising of crops in China, they usually think of wide green cool rice paddies and several diligent oxen. The average Chinese farmer holds from two to five acres of land, which he keeps at high productivity level

146

through his own unfailing strength and energy, natural fertilization, and the rotation of crops. He is seldom able to raise even one ox upon his lands. Through force of circumstances he has had to use instinct and intelligence to become expert at extreme economy. He not only raises 2 to 3 crops a year on the same field, but he often has more than one crop growing on the same piece of land at the same time. So, as one crop is ripening, the next crop is being sowed in between, and as the first crop is cut, the second is ripening, and the third crop is being sowed. Yet his sense of economy does not leave him content with just his land; he must, in his spare moments, indulge in water farming. He utilizes every near-by pond, brook, stream, or lake. These he uses not only for fishing, but also for raising water chestnuts, lotus stems, and other edible water vegetables. In his home he cultivates bean sprouts, for this vegetable flourishes upon racks that are kept moist through proper drainage, and yet uses no precious space upon his farmland.

In raising plants, the Chinese farmer prefers to grow those that will take the least space and yet serve more than one purpose. Many varieties of legumes are planted, especially soya beans. The bean, besides fertilizing the soil as it develops, offers an extensive assortment of products, namely, oil, sauce, bean curd, soya milk, and so on. The bamboo also offers innumerable uses. Its young shoots serve as food, its foliage as material for paper and clothing, and its stalks as substance for building. Then also, the sacred lotus (water lily) is highly regarded by the Chinese as both a decorative and a utilitarian plant. It is the symbol of purity and perfection, for it grows out of mud but remains undefiled. Its gigantic blossoms of pink-tipped ivory are tuliplike, and its rich green leaves float platterlike upon the still waters. Every part of the plant has a name and a use. The regal blossom 荷花 haw-faah is used as an ornament. The creeping jointed underwater stems 藕根 ngow-gun when cut across expose a series of hollow tunnels concentrically arranged in solid tissue. These stems, fresh or dried, are sliced and

147

cooked for food; and, when dried and ground to powder, are used as arrowroot 藕粉 *ngow-fun*. The leaves when dried are used for wrapping food, but when these *haw-yeep* 荷葉 are fresh, they may be used to add flavor and fragrance to cooking food. The stalk, 藕鼻 *haw-bay*, and its receptacle in the shape of a watering can nozzle 蓮蓬 *lien-poong*, are ground and used medicinally. The fruits 蓮實 *lien-sut*, the seeds 蓮子 *lien-jee*, and the kernels 蓮薏 *lien-yee* are generally eaten in festival foods; and, the dried yellow stamens 蓮鬚 *lien-so* are used as a cosmetic of astringent quality.

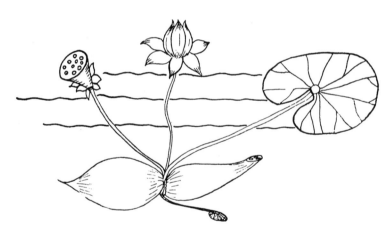

The sacred lotus, symbol of purity and perfection

芽菜炒猪肉

Ngaah Choy Chow Jüh Yook   Pea Sprouts Braised Pork

¼ lb. loin pork   1 clove garlic
1 lb. fresh pea sprouts   1½ tsp. cornstarch
2 stalks celery   2 tsp. soya sauce
1 onion   1 tsp. sugar
½ cup sugar peas (mange tout)   ¾ tsp. salt
¼ cup wun yee (cloud ears)   ¼ tsp. pepper
                    1 tbls. salad oil

Slice pork fine and mix with 1 teaspoon soya sauce, ½ teaspoon cornstarch, ½ teaspoon sugar, ¼ teaspoon salt, and pepper, and salad oil. Smash a clove of garlic and store neatly on top of meat. Make a cornstarch mixture of 1 teaspoon cornstarch, 2 tablespoons water, ½ teaspoon sugar, and 1 teaspoon soya sauce. Soak and clean *wun yee* thoroughly. Slice celery fine diagonally. Slice onion into fine wedges. Wash and clean pea sprouts of their jackets, and remove their roots.

Heat a little oil in a large frying pan, add onion and fry until the wedges separate into layers easily, then add celery, sugar peas, pea sprouts, and *wun yee*. Fry 2 minutes, add ½ teaspoon salt, stir constantly, then cover pan with lid and let vegetables braise another 2 minutes (until the vegetables are almost cooked). Remove to clean dish.

Toss garlic into frying pan, add pork mixture, stir and fry ½ minute, cover pan with lid and braise pork 3 minutes. Add braised vegetables, mix well, stir a hole in center of ingredients, pour in cornstarch mixture, and when it is heated and slightly thickened, stir it well into other ingredients. Cover pan with lid and braise all ingredients together 2 to 3 minutes more. Then serve.

豆 炒 猪 肉

Dow Chow Jüh Yook — Lima Beans Braised with Pork

4 lbs. lima beans in pods
½ lb. loin pork
2 slices smoked ham
2 slices bacon
2 tbls. diced fat pork
½ tsp. salt

½ tsp. cornstarch
2 cloves garlic
1 large piece ginger
2 tbls. soya sauce
1 cup broth or hot water

Shell lima bean pods and remove outer leathery skin of each bean. Fine-dice ham, bacon, fat pork, and lean loin pork. Mix diced loin pork with cornstarch. Chop ginger and garlic.

Heat a little oil in a frying pan, fry ginger and garlic until golden. Add fat pork, bacon, and then loin pork. Add soya sauce and scramble ingredients during 2 minutes of frying. Remove ingredients to dish. Using same pan, fry lima beans, and then add broth or water, and salt. Cover pan with a lid and braise beans about 10 minutes. Add ham and fried pork mixture. Fry ingredients another 2 to 3 minutes and serve.

辣 椒 醬

Laat Jew Jeung — Chilied Mince Meat

1 doz. haah maai (Chinese dried shrimps)
¼ lb. slab of semilean bacon
1 large green bell pepper
1 large red bell pepper
½ tbls. sugar

2 cloves garlic
6 tiny red-hot chiles or 1-3 tsp. hot chile powder
3 tbls. saang see jeung (Chinese aromatic sauce)

Remove seeds and membranes from bell peppers. Dice into ½-inch squares. Fine-dice bacon. Mince shrimps after soaking them until soft. Crush garlic. Chop red-hot chiles coarse. Make a sauce of *saang see jeung*, sugar, and ½ cup hot water.

Heat a little oil in a frying pan. Fry garlic, bell peppers, bacon, shrimps, and chile. Cover pot with lid and braise ingredients 2 minutes. Add sauce, blend thoroughly into other ingredients, cover pan with lid, and braise all together over low fire for 20 minutes.

Variations can be achieved with this dish by adding ingredients. A favorite variation is created by the addition of fried cubes of bean curd. Take cake of fresh bean curd, dice into ½-inch cubelets, fry in deep fat until golden and then add to cooked chile mixture.

番茄炒牛肉

Faahn Keh Chow Ngow Yook	Tomato Braised with Beef

4 *large firm red tomatoes*	1 *tbls. vinegar*
1 *large potato*	½ *tbls. sugar*
1 *onion*	½ *tsp. salt*
1 *green bell pepper*	¼ *tsp. pepper*
½ *lb. tender beef*	1 *tbls. vegetable oil*
1 *clove garlic*	1 *tbls. cornstarch*

Peel and slice potatoes very thin. Fry chips in deep fat until a golden brown and drain. Cut tomatoes and onions into 8 wedges. Slice bell pepper into coarse strips. Slice beef and mix with ½ teaspoon cornstarch, ¼ teaspoon salt, ½ teaspoon sugar, pepper, and vegetable oil. Make cornstarch mixture of remainder of cornstarch, 1 teaspoon sugar, vinegar, ¼ teaspoon salt, and a little water. Crush clove of garlic.

Heat a little oil in a frying pan, fry onions and bell pepper.

151

Cover pan with a lid and braise onions and pepper until tender yet fresh. Add the tomatoes and continue braising 1 to 2 minutes. Remove to dish.

Toss garlic into frying pan, fry ½ minute and then add beef mixture. Fry and toss beef around and when it is still rather rare, add vegetables. Stir a hollow in center of ingredients, pour in cornstarch mixture, allow to heat up and thicken slightly before stirring into other ingredients. Cover pan with lid, braise ingredients 1 to 2 minutes. In the meanwhile, arrange potato chips in a ring along outer edge of serving dish, place tomato-beef mixture neatly in hollow and serve.

霉菜蒸肉餅

Mooi Choy Jing Yook Bang   Pickled Cabbage Steamed with Pork

1–2 heads pickled cabbage° (1 cup)	*½ lb. minced pork*
3 sprigs Chinese parsley	*1 small piece* gwaw pay
¼ cup cloud ears (wun yee)	*(dried tangerine skin)*
6 water chestnuts	*½ tbls. soya sauce*
2 large Chinese mushrooms	*½ tsp. sugar*
¼ tsp. pepper	*1 tsp. cornstarch*
¼ tsp. salt	*1 tbls. salad oil*
¼ cup cold water	

Mince all ingredients fine and mix with condiments, oil, and water. Arrange in one large serving dish or two smaller dishes. Steam about 30 minutes, until pork is done.

° Pickled cabbage comes in several varieties. The most easily obtained in Chinese grocery shops are *haahm choy, choong choy,* and *muy choy.*

茶 瓜 蒸 猪 肉

Chaah Gwaah Jing Jüh Yook   Tea Melons Steamed with Pork

½ lb. loin pork slightly fat   ¼ tsp. pepper
3 large pieces chaah gwaah (little   ½ tsp. salt
   golden tea melons)   ¼ tsp. sugar
1 tbls. soya sauce   1 tsp. cornstarch
                  1 tbls. vegetable oil

Slice pork fine. Slice *chaah gwaah* into 2-inch lengths. (Three
pieces of *chaah gwaah* equal about ½ cup of slices.) Mix pork and
chaah gwaah with soya sauce, pepper, salt, sugar, cornstarch, and
oil. Squeeze and blend ingredients together. Arrange in dish and
steam about 30 to 40 minutes.

蘿 蔔 炒 牛 肉

Law Baak Chow Ngow Yook   Turnips Braised with Beef

2 snow-white long turnips   1 tbls. saang see jeung
4 scallions   1 tsp. sugar
1 clove garlic   1½ tsp. soya sauce
1 slice ginger   ½ tbls. cornstarch
¼ lb. tender beef   1 tbls. vegetable oil
¼ tsp. salt   1 pinch pepper

Boil turnips until tender, drain, and peel. Slice turnips into
strips about ⅛-inch thick. Chop scallions into 1-inch lengths. Mince
ginger and garlic. Slice beef, mix with *saang see jeung*, ½ teaspoon
sugar, 1 teaspoon soya sauce, ½ teaspoon cornstarch, ¼ teaspoon salt,
and a pinch of pepper, and oil. Make a mixture of 1 teaspoon cornstarch, ¼ cup water, ½ teaspoon sugar, and ½ teaspoon soya sauce.

153

Heat a little oil in a frying pan, toss in scallions, turnips, and salt, and fry 2 minutes. Remove to dish. Toss garlic and ginger into frying pan, add beef, fry a few seconds, and then stir in turnips. Stir a hollow in center of ingredients, pour in cornstarch mixture, and when heated and slightly thickened, mix with other ingredients. Cover pan with lid, braise beef and turnips 1 to 2 minutes, then serve.

炒 肉 鬆

Chow Yook Soong   Fried Tasty Meat Mince

½ cup peanuts or almonds	1 tbls. dry sherry
8 water chestnuts	2 tbls. soya sauce
4 Chinese mushrooms	1 tbls. cornstarch
¼ cup sugar peas	½ tsp. sugar
2 stalks celery	½ tsp. salt
2 slices ginger	¼ tsp. pepper
1 clove garlic	1 tbls. vegetable oil
½ lb. minced pork	1 small head lettuce

Shell peanuts or blanch almonds, and fry in a little hot oil until golden. Drain, cool, and crush to a mince. Dice water chestnuts, mushrooms, sugar peas, and celery very fine. Mix pork with 1 tablespoon soya sauce, 1 teaspoon cornstarch, ¼ teaspoon salt, pepper, and sugar, and 2 tablespoons water. Make mixture of wine, 1 tablespoon soya sauce, 2 teaspoons cornstarch, a pinch of sugar, and ¼ cup soaked mushroom water.

Heat a little oil in a frying pan, fry all fine-diced ingredients, sprinkle with ¼ teaspoon salt, cover with lid, and braise 3 minutes. Remove to dish. Fry garlic and ginger, add pork mixture, scramble a minute, then braise 2 minutes. Add vegetables; stir until well mixed. Arrange a hollow in center of ingredients, pour in sauce, heat until slightly thickened, then blend into other ingredients.

Cover pan with lid and braise ingredients about 3 minutes longer or until pork is well cooked.

In the meanwhile, coarsely chop up lettuce and braise in very little oil and light sprinkling of salt. When tender, add to minced vegetable-meat mixture. Arrange in dish, sprinkle with nuts, and serve.

蠔油豆腐

Ho Yow Dow Fooh   Oyster Sauce Bean Curds

    2 cakes fresh bean curd   *1 clove garlic*
    3 stalks scallions   *3 tbls. oyster sauce*
    ¼ cup parsley leaves   *½ tsp. salt*

Cut bean curd cakes into pieces about ½ inch by 1 inch by 1 inch. Chop scallions. Heat about ½ inch of oil and fry pieces of bean curds to light golden hue. Drain.

Heat a little oil in a frying pan, fry garlic, add bean curd, sprinkle with salt and oyster sauce, and about 2 tablespoons boiling water. Stir and mix, then sprinkle bean curds with scallions and parlsey leaves. Cover pan with lid, braise ingredients 2 minutes, and serve.

番瓜炒牛肉

Faahn Gwaah Chow Ngow Yook   Squash Braised with Beef

    4 squashes   *1 tbls. soya sauce*
    ¼ lb. beef   *½ tsp. cornstarch*
    1 tbls. dow see (black spiced beans) *¼ tsp. salt*
    1 slice ginger   *1 pinch pepper*
    1 clove garlic   *1 tbls. salad oil*

Slice squash coarsely. Slice beef and mix with crushed *dow see*, 1 tablespoon water, and minced garlic. Heat a little oil in a frying pan, fry ginger, and then add squash. Fry a moment and then pour ¼ cup water over vegetables. Cover pan with lid and braise squash about 15 minutes. Add soya sauce, cornstarch, salt, pepper, and oil to beef mixture. Set this beef mixture carefully upon squash, cover frying pan with lid, and braise contents another 5 to 10 minutes. Mix beef with squash just before taking pan off fire. Serve.

芥蘭炒义烧

Gaai Laan Chow Chaah Sieu   Broccoli Braised with Roast Pork

½ lb. tender young broccoli	1 clove garlic
½ lb. sliced chaah sieu (roast pork)	1 slice ginger
1 tsp. sugar	1 tbls. sherry
¼ tsp. salt	1 tsp. cornstarch
2 tbls. soya sauce	

Cut tender stems of broccoli into 1½-inch lengths. Use the young leaves and the flowers also. Peel tougher stems and split almost through, lengthwise. Mince ginger and crush garlic. Slice Chinese roast pork. Heat a little oil in a frying pan, fry broccoli, then add ginger and garlic. Sprinkle with salt and sugar. Cover pan with lid and braise 3 to 5 minutes, until broccoli is cooked, but yet crisp and green. In the meanwhile, stir cornstarch, a little water, wine, and soya sauce into a mixture. Stir a hollow in center of frying ingredients, pour sauce into hollow, and when hot and slightly thickened, blend into broccoli. Cover pan with lid and braise contents another 5 to 10 minutes. Add *chaah sieu*, fry together a moment and serve.

豆角炒猪肉

Dow Gock Chow Jüh Yook   Cow Peas Braised with Pork

½ lb. cow peas (string beans)   1 tsp. soya sauce
¼ lb. slightly fat loin pork   ½ tsp. cornstarch
2 slices ginger   ½ tsp. sugar
1 clove garlic   ¼ tsp. pepper
½ tsp. salt   1 tbls. vegetable oil

String beans and cut in halves. Slice pork and mix with soya sauce, cornstarch, sugar, ¼ teaspoon salt, pepper, and vegetable oil. Heat a little oil in a frying pan, fry minced garlic and chopped ginger, then the beans. Sprinkle vegetables with ¼ teaspoon salt. Fry 2 minutes, add pork mixture, and ¼ cup boiling water. Cover pan with lid, and braise contents slowly about 15 minutes. Serve.

五花肉炆笋

Ngung Faah Yook Mun Sün   Salted Bamboo Braised with Pork

½ lb. ngung faah yook (five-flowered   1 tsp. soya sauce
   pork)   ¼ tsp. sugar
1½ cups dried bamboo shoots   ¼ tsp. pepper
1½ tbls. naam yü sauce   ½ tsp. salt
1 clove garlic   1 tbls. vegetable oil
            1 tsp. cornstarch

Slice five-flowered pork into thin ⅛-inch-thick strips. Mix with naam yü sauce, soya sauce, salt, pepper, sugar, cornstarch, and oil. Heat a little oil in a pot, fry garlic and pork mixture about 3 minutes. Cut soaked and softened dried bamboo shoots into 2-inch lengths and add them to frying meat. Fry together about 2 minutes, then add enough boiling water to reach two thirds the height of ingredients. Cover pot with lid and simmer contents slowly about 1 to 1½ hours, or until both meat and bamboo shoots are extremely tender.

襄苦瓜

Yeung Fooh Gwaah   Bitter Melon Stuffed with Meat

4 medium-sized bitter melons, fooh   1 tbls. soya sauce
    gwaah (balsam pears)   2 tsp. cornstarch
½ lb. minced pork   ½ tsp. sugar
1 clove garlic   ¼ tsp. pepper
2 scallions   ½ tsp. salt
¼ cup Chinese parsley leaves   1 tbls. vegetable oil
            1 tbls. dow see (black spiced beans)

Mince scallions, and crush ½ clove garlic. Mix pork with soya sauce, cornstarch, sugar, pepper, salt, oil, crushed garlic, parsley leaves, and minced scallions. Cut bitter melon into 1½-inch-thick disks, then using sharp instrument, cut out white inner pulp. Stuff these hollowed out disks firmly with meat mixture until filling bulges out on both sides with a slight convex. Meat has a tendency to shrink during cooking.

Heat about 1/16 inch of oil in a frying pan, fry stuffed disks on both sides until the meat acquires a rich golden brown. Add a sauce made of ½ clove garlic crushed with dow see and diluted with ½ cup boiling water. Cover pan with lid and braise contents slowly about 20 minutes. Serve.

茄炒猪肉

Keh Chow Jüh Yook   Eggplant Braised with Pork

1 firm eggplant   ½ tsp. sugar
½ lb. slightly fat loin pork   ¼ tsp. pepper
1 clove garlic   ½ tsp. salt
2 tbls. saang see jeung sauce   1 tsp. cornstarch
1 tsp. soya sauce   1 slice ginger

Peel eggplant and cut into pieces about 2″ x 1″ x ½″. Slice ginger fine. Heat a little oil in a frying pan, fry the ginger, add eggplant, sprinkle with ½ teaspoon salt, and fry together about 2 minutes. Remove to dish.

Slice pork and mix with crushed garlic, crushed *saang see jeung*, soya sauce, sugar, salt, pepper, and cornstarch. Heat a little oil in frying pan and fry pork mixture a moment. Add ½ cup boiling water, cover pan with lid and braise pork 8 to 10 minutes. Add eggplant and braise another 5 to 10 minutes.

Chapter IX

RICE AND MIEN DISHES

IN CHINESE, *waw* 和 harmony and peace is a character which reveals the truthful thought of the universal mind, the knowledge that man cannot exist peacefully and in harmony with his fellowmen unless he first feels at peace with his own stomach. The word is a written combination of characters which first symbolizes staple food through the similar phonetic word *waw* 禾 growing grain, and then depicts man's necessity to eat and be nourished by food through the word *hao* 口 mouth.

As far back as the Early Neolithic Culture (20,000 to 5000 B. C.) grain cultivation was in existence in China through a system of stone-blade hoeing on large areas of cleared lands. The importance of grain foods is shown by many pictographical words of the Yin Period (1400 B. C.). For example, the word meaning year is a picture combination representing a sheaf of growing grain and a man; and the word for harvest is exemplified by the threshing of a sheaf of grain by man.

Rice, today, is the staple food of China, although there is a more marked consumption of wheat and millet in the northern provinces. Rice comes under a varying number of names according to the type of grain and the stage of its preparation. The hulled rice is called *muy* 米 a picturesque word depicting separation of

Yin Period pictographs representing plowing, year, harvest

grain 米 . Cooked rice is called *faahn* 饭 and rice soup (congee) is called *jook* 粥. Glutinous rice is called *naw-muy* 糯米 and when it comes in powder form it is called *naw-muy fun* 糯米饭. The long-grain rice grown in the Carolinas is the best type for making plain rice and rice dishes.

In order to teach the pricelessness and preciousness of rice, innumerable proverbs and superstition have developed concerning this grain. The upsetting of a rice bowl is an omen of ill fortune, and no insult can be greater and no greater calamity can be caused in any home than when an intruder deliberately snatches away a bowl of rice and empties its contents upon the ground. The wasting of rice is discouraged by the warning children receive that for each grain left in their rice bowl a pock mark will appear on the face of their future bride. Or, as my grandmother used to say, "There are over 450,000,000 people in our country. If each were to leave a grain of rice each day, just think of the waste!"

Mien 麵 noodles, called the staple food of the north, is made from a combination of wheat and beans. They come in a great number of forms, such as flat lengths, round narrow lengths, tubular lengths, and a transparent variety called *fun-see* 粉絲 "powdered silk," which some people so aptly translate by their appearance as "cellophane noodles."

Because of their great length, *mien* are a symbol of longevity. They are generally served at birthdays and feast days, and the guests are required to partake of this dish in large portions, thus signifying their desire to wish long life and happiness to the person in whose honor the party is given.

白飯

Baak Faahn   White Rice

Measure ½ cup of rice for each man, and ¼ to ⅓ cup of rice for each woman. Then use 1½ to 2 cups water for each cup of washed rice to be cooked (short-grain rice needs less water t han long-grain rice). Those who prefer the Cantonese cooked rice (quite hard) use 1 cup water to 1 cup rice, and a shorter cooking period. Wash rice until rinsing water is clear. Add water, bring the water to boil, drop in ½ teaspoon butter (this is merely a precaution to keep the rice from boiling over), turn down flame to very low, cover pot with lid, and allow rice to cook slowly and undisturbed until done. Never, never stir the rice! Refrain from peeking to see how the rice is coming along during the first 20 minutes of the cooking. After that time, you may peek, for the rice cooking time varies according to the amount of rice used. Two cups of rice generally take about 40 minutes to cook. Anyhow, after the first 20 minutes of cooking it is quite permissible to take a peek into the pot at infrequent intervals. If the rice on top is flaky and cooked through, and if natural steam holes are formed in the dull dry surface of the snow-white mound of individual grains of rice, then the rice is ready.

炒 飯

Chow Faahn   Fried Rice

4 cups boiled rice at least   1 tsp. salt
    one day old   ¼ tsp. pepper
3 eggs   ½ cup sliced chaah sieu
4 scallions   (Chinese roast pork)
1 cup parsley leaves   2 tbls. soya sauce

Dice *chaah sieu*. Chop scallions. Beat eggs. Heat a little oil in
a frying pan, toss in rice. Fry rice until hot, stir and gently press out
all the lumps. Add scallions, salt, pepper, and *chaah sieu*. When
thoroughly mixed, stir a hollow in center of rice, break in 3 eggs
and scramble. When semicooked, stir into rice until blended. Stir
in parsley leaves, sprinkle with soya sauce. Serve.

Fried Rice No. 2

4 cups boiled rice at least   6 eggs
    one day old   1 tsp. salt
6 scallions   ½ tsp. pepper
1 bell pepper   ¼ clove garlic minced
2 slices ginger   1 pinch pepper
½ cup parsley leaves   ¼ tsp. salt
4 slices ham   ½ tsp. cornstarch
2 slices bacon   ½ tsp. sugar
⅛ lb. fillet of beef   2 tbls. soya sauce
                5 tbls. vegetable oil

Julienne bell pepper and ginger fine, slice scallions, and dice
ham and bacon. Slice fillet of beef paper thin and mix with its ac-

163

companying ingredients of garlic, pepper, salt, cornstarch, sugar, 1 tablespoon soya sauce, and 1 tablespoon oil.

Heat 4 tablespoons oil in large skillet, fry ginger and bell peppers with salt and pepper 1 minute. Break in rice. When grains are hot and separated, stir a hole in center, toss in ham, bacon, and scallions, fry a moment, and then mix into rice thoroughly. Stir another hole in center of rice, drop in beef mixture, fry ½ minute, add parsley leaves, fry another ½ minute, and then mix thoroughly into rice. Stir still another hole in center of rice, drop in eggs, fry until semisolid, and then mix into rice. Sprinkle with 1 tablespoon soya sauce and serve. Garnish with parsley leaves if desired.

猪 肉 粥

Jüh Yook Jook   Pork Congee

1½ cups raw rice	1 cup parsley leaves
½ lb. loin pork	6 scallions chopped
2 tbls. oil	1 small piece choong choy
1 gal. boiling water	(pickled cabbage—optional)
1 piece ginger	1 tbls. salt
1 piece gwaw pay	1 tsp. sugar
(dried tangerine skin)	¼ tsp. pepper

Mix rice with 1 tablespoon oil and 2 teaspoons salt. Place in large pot and then pour in 4 quarts boiling water. Cover pot with lid and bring water to quick boil. Throw *gwaw pay* into water. Shred ginger fine and add to pot also. Simmer 1½ hours.

In the meanwhile, mince pork, blend with 1 tablespoon oil, 1 teaspoon salt, 1 teaspoon sugar, pepper, and minced *choong choy*. Add meat mixture to congee, simmer 20 minutes more. Then add parsley leaves and scallions. Simmer 5 to 10 minutes, then serve.

One egg per person may be dropped in 5 minutes or less before serving.

烧 鴨 粥

Sieu Ngaap Jook   Roast Duck Congee

Bones, lower legs, wings, and neck of   1½ cups raw rice
    one roast duck   4 qts. boiling water
3 pieces of gon yiu chee (dried scal-   2 tbls. vegetable oil
    lops)   1 tbls. salt
1 small piece gwaw pay (dried tan-   1 small piece of ginger
    gerine skin)   6 scallions
                                                               1 cup parsley leaves

Heat gallon of water with *gon yiu chee* and *gwaw pay*. Mix rice with oil and salt, and add to boiling water. After ½ hour add duck and ginger sliced thin. Simmer under lid for 1½ to 2 hours. Five minutes before serving, sprinkle surface with choped scallions and parsley leaves. Add salt to taste. Serve.

HOW TO PREPARE NOODLES OR MIEN

Prepare a large pot of swiftly boiling water. Drop in sufficient *mien* or noodles for persons to be served, figuring on about ¼ pound per person. Boil noodles about 3 minutes, turn into colander, run through cold water, then drain. When the *mien* or noodles are thoroughly drained, use them either for soup or for frying.

長壽麵

| Cheung Sao Mien | Long Life Noodles |

5 lbs. Chinese egg noodles	3 tbls. soya sauce
(sufficient for 20 persons)	1 tsp. salt
½ lb. sugar peas (mange tout)	1 tsp. sugar
2 onions	½ tsp. pepper
6 stalks celery	2 cloves garlic
2 large Chinese mushrooms	2 thick slices ginger
2 lbs. bean sprouts	3 eggs for garnish
½ lb. loin pork	4 slices smoked ham for garnish
1 lb. fillet of chicken	1 tablespoon vegetable oil
3 tbls. cornstarch	1¾ cups water

Slice peas, onions, celery, and mushrooms. Slice pork and chicken and mix with 1 tablespoon cornstarch, 1 tablespoon soya sauce, pepper, ½ teaspoon salt, sugar, 1 tablespoon vegetable oil, and ¼ cup water. Make sauce of 1½ cups water, 2 tablespoons soya sauce, 2 tablespoons cornstarch, and the ginger minced very, very fine.

Prepare noodles by plunging in boiling water, boiling for 3 minutes and then draining until thoroughly dry. Divide noodles in small portions and fry each portion in a little hot oil until a rich golden hue. If more oil is needed to prevent sticking during the process of frying, add the oil along inner edge of frying pan. Never pour oil directly upon noodles. It will only make them greasy and be absorbed.

When all noodles are fried, heat a little oil in a frying pan and fry vegetables. Sprinkle vegetables with 1 teaspoon salt, cover pan with lid, and braise vegetables 2 to 3 minutes. Remove to dish. Fry garlic, add meat mixture, stir and fry a while and then add braised vegetables. Mix ingredients together, form a hollow in

166

center, and pour sauce into that hollow. Cover pot with lid, braise 1 minute, and then add noodles. Mix all together carefully so as not to break noodles, fry another 3 minutes, and serve. Decorate with ham cut into matchlike strips, parsley leaves, and egg-flower garnish. (See page 92.)

伊府麵

Ieh Fooh Mien   Ieh Fooh Noodles

½ lb. ieh fooh mien, a thread-   ½ tsp. sugar
    like ochre-colored vermicelli°   1 tsp. soya sauce
¼ lb. minced pork   ¼ tsp. pepper
1 firm red tomato   ½ tsp. cornstarch
1 clove garlic   1 tsp. vegetable oil
½ Spanish onion   ½ tsp. salt
        1½ quarts chicken broth

Mix pork with sugar, salt, pepper, cornstarch, soya sauce, 2 table-spoons water, and oil. Scald tomato and peel off skin. Mince tomato. Mince-dice onion.

Heat 2 inches of vegetable oil and fry noodles to rich golden hue. Drain.

Heat a very little oil in a pot, fry ½ teaspoon salt, garlic, and onion for a few moments. Add chicken broth and diced tomatoes, cover pot with lid, and simmer contents for 10 minutes. Stir in minced pork, cover pot and simmer 5 minutes. Add the *mien* and simmer 10 to 15 minutes. Serve.

° If Chinese *ieh fooh mien* cannot be obtained at a Chinese grocery shop, try to purchase the Italian or Mexican variety of vermicelli. They are almost identical and make a most delicious substitute.

167

THE JOY OF CHINESE COOKING

湯 麵

Tong Mien   Broth Noodles

1 lb. noodles	½ lb. spinach
1½ qts. chicken broth	1 tbls. soya sauce
¼ lb. fillet of chicken	¾ tsp. salt
½ cup bamboo shoots	1 tbls. oil
4 Chinese mushroms	2 slices smoked ham
¼ tsp. pepper	¼ tsp. sugar

Plunge noodles into swiftly boiling water, boil 2 minutes, drain, and then toss into chicken broth with ½ teaspoon salt. Slice chicken and mix with ¼ teaspoon salt, pepper, sugar, and 1 teaspoon soya sauce. Heat a little oil in a pan and fry chicken a moment. Dice bamboo shoots and slice mushrooms. Add bamboo shoots, mushrooms, and spinach to chicken. Sprinkle with 2 teaspoons soya sauce.

Pour soup and noodles into large serving bowl or many individual bowls. Place mixed ingredients over noodles, garnish with minced ham, and serve.

Chapter X

CHINESE DESSERTS

THE EIGHT TREASURES

Baat Bo 八寶 or the Eight Treasures are represented by eight objects which, when exposed with the mystic knot or the red cord, are believed to symbolize and possess effective charm. The symbols for the Eight Treasures are: 1. the Dragon Pearl; 2. the Golden Coin; 3. the Lozenge; 4. the Mirror; 5. the Stone Chime; 6. Books; 7. Rhinocerous Horns; and, 8. the Artemisia Leaf.

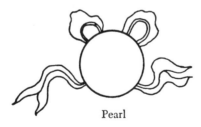

Pearl

Ancient fables relate that the pearl is created by the essence of moon, which distilled by the mysterious elements of nature comes to life within the shell of a mollusk. Entwined by a cord of red, it becomes a charm against the evils of fire.

Chinese cash or coins are symbols of prosperity, and when entwined by a cord of red, serve as an amulet for warding off evil.

Coin

The coin has a square hole in the center, which signifies the integrity of those who come in contact with it by depicting the character as "square within and round without."

Lozenge

The Lozenge is usually a diamond shaped or rectangularly shaped open frame draped with a red cord. Often used as a head ornament, it is a symbol of victory.

Mirror

170

Made of polished bronze mixed with an alloy of tin, the circular mirrors were the earliest in China. The backs were beautifully embossed with designs, and in the center there were projections perforated for the purpose of passing through a silken cord. The mirror symbolizes unceasing conjugal happiness. It is also supposed to reveal hidden spirits and the secrets of the future. Mirrors are hung in doorways and by bedsides for the purpose of preventing evil; for, it is said, that if it so happens that an undesirable spirit approaches the mirror and sees himself reflected, he will become so frightened by his own gruesome image that he will rush off without delay.

Stone Chime

The Stone Chime is generally made of jade. It is an instrument of percussion. Phonetically the word possesses the same sound as the word meaning "happiness," and thus has become a symbol of felicity.

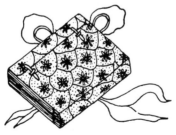

Books

The symbol of two books decorated by a cord is also regarded as an amulet to ward off evil spirits. Scholastic achievements are

171

greatly venerated, and admired in China; and, it is said that those who are full of book learning need not fear the presence of spirits.

Rhinocerous Horns

Carved with exquisite designs and ornamented with the mystic bow, Rhinocerous Horns signify happiness. They were used in ages past as drinking vessels, and their supposed power of sweating should there be the presence of poison in the liquid made them indispensable in every court.

Artemisia Leaf

The Artemisia Leaf resting upon a cord is used as a sign of felicity and a protection against evil. It is often hung in front of doorways and possesses such fragrance that its exudation of perfume is supposed to disperse demons and malign spirits.

八寶飯

Baat Bo Faahn   Eight-Treasure Rice

1 *lb. glutinous rice* (naw muy)	*½ cup* lien jee *(lotus seeds)*
½ cup ground suet	*½ cup* loong ngaan *(dragon eyes)*°
¼ cup sugar	8 ching muy *(Chinese plums)*°
2 tbls. barley	*¼ cup candied orange peel*
½ cup honeyed dates	*¼ cup green candied fruit*
¼ cup candied cherries	*½ cup almonds or walnuts*

Boil glutinous rice until water is evaporated, then carefully mix in suet and sugar. Continue cooking rice very slowly until almost done. In the meanwhile, blanch lotus seeds and nuts. When lotus seeds are blanched, cook with barley. Pit all fruits and cut larger into quarters and smaller into halves. Slice candied fruit into narrow strips.

Oil mold heavily with lard, and cover with thin layer of glutinous rice. Place some fruit and nuts in attractive rows or designs upon layer of rice, and then press well into the surface so that they might show through later on. For the sake of effect, balance the colors or the fruits and nuts while arranging them. Over this carefully place another layer of rice alternately with another layer of fruits and nuts. End with layer of rice. Place mold in steamer, and steam about 30 to 40 minutes. Turn pudding out on a hot platter and serve steaming hot.

° If *loong ngaan* cannot be easily obtained (comes in cans), then use raisins instead; and, if *ching muy* cannot be purchased, then just use ordinary stewing prunes.

杏仁茶

Hung Yun Chaah   Genuine Almond Tea

> 4 *cups blanched almonds*   ¾ *cup raw rice*
> 3 *qts. cold water*   2 *tsp. vanilla*
> ½ *cup sugar*   ⅛ *tsp. salt*

Place almonds and rice grains in stone bowl and grind with a pestle to pulp. Add water and allow mixture to soak 1 hour. Stir thoroughly and then strain liquid through cheesecloth. Tie remaining pulp in the cheesecloth and milk thoroughly by squeezing every available drop into pot of liquid. Allow liquid to simmer slowly in double boiler or very heavy metal pot. Hang the cheesecloth bag of almond-rice pulp in the liquid. At times, milk contents into the pot. Stir frequently during the three hours of cooking. Almond tea should thicken to a medium gravy. Add sugar, salt, and vanilla. Bring almond tea to quick boil just before serving.

杏仁糊

Hung Yun Woo   Mock Almond Lake

> 1 *can evaporated milk*   ½ *tsp. vanilla extract*
> 2 *qts. water*   ¼ *cup cornstarch*
> 1 *tbls. almond extract*   ¼ *cup sugar*

Boil water and evaporated milk. Slowly stir in cornstarch dissolved in cold water. When thickened, add almond extract, vanilla extract, and sugar. Stir and simmer slowly until cooked (20 minutes). Serve.

CHINESE DESERTS

鷄蛋糕

Ghuy Daahn Go   Chinese Sponge Cake

6 eggs   ¼ tsp. baking powder
4 tbls. sugar   8 tsp. water
½ cup sifted flour   1 tbls. lemon or vanilla essence

Sift flour, measure ½ cup and add baking powder. Sift the two
ingredients several times. Line layer cake pan about 8″ x 8″ with
oiled paper. Heat about 4 inches of water in very large steamer,
for recipe makes enough batter for 1 large steamed cake.

Separate yolks carefully from egg whites. Beat egg whites until
stiff but not dry. Add sugar and water to egg yokes and beat them
together with a whipper for at least ½ hour (do not use an egg
beater or an electric machine). Sift flour into egg yolk mixture,
which is extremely fluffy and almost stiff enough to hold its shape.
Beat together until blended, then add essence, and fold in
egg white. Beat in a whipping motion and a folding motion alternately for 1 minute. Pour batter into pan and place in steamer.
Place a cloth over mouth of pot under lid to catch steam drippings.
Steam about 25 minutes. To test doneness, prick cake with straw.
If no batter adheres to straw and cake shrinks slightly, pulling at
oiled paper, cake is done. Turn cake out upon a rack to unsteam
itself and cool. Cut and serve hot.

芝蔴餅

Jieh Maah Baang   Sesame Seed Cakes

2 cups flour   ½ cup sesame seeds
½ cup strained suet (pork)   ½ tsp. baking powder
½ cup sugar   2 eggs

175

Sift flour and baking powder onto pastry board. Stir a hollow in center and pour in sugar, break in 1 egg, and drop in lard. Using your fingers, gently work flour into mixture until a dough is formed. Add a very little water if necessary. Knead dough gently in a pushing-away-with-the-palm and pulling-up-with-the-fingers and folding-the-dough-back-over motion. Roll dough into long sausage about ½-inch thick in diameter, and with knife, cut off ½-inch-wide segments. Roll each piece into ball with palms of hands and press it flat into ¼-inch-thick disk. Beat an egg yolk, and brush surface of each disk lightly with yolk. Then drop disks, wet side down, upon sesame seeds. Press sesame seeds gently into dough. Brush surface lightly with egg white. Place disks on lightly greased baking sheet, sesame-seed side up, and bake in moderate oven about 15 minutes.

脆蔴花

Chûy Mow Faah   Crisp Mow Flowers

2 cups flour	1 egg
½ cup strained pork suet	Water if necessary
½ cup sugar	Vegetable oil for deep fat frying

Sift flour onto pastry board. Stir heap to form a hollow in center. Pour in sugar, drop in solid strained suet, and break in egg. Blend ingredients gently with fingers until a stiffer than medium dough is achieved. Add ice cold water if necessary.

Heat about 2 inches of oil in pan. Roll dough into sausage about 1 inch in diameter. Cut off 1-inch pieces. Roll each piece into long ribbon about 9 inches long. Double ribbon in half and twist the two strands several times. Then bring the two ends up and pass through the loop at the opposite end of the twists, where the ribbon was doubled in two. Place these twisted Mow Flowers carefully

176

in hot oil and fry until fluffed out to capacity (2 to 3 times original size) and of an orange-golden brown color. Drain and serve cold.

Peiping Dust

In the ancient city of *Peiping*, where honor, peace, and courtesy reign, all the gems of exquisite art may be found. Formerly the home of emperors and princes, it was called *Peking*, "Northern Capital." Now with its remaining splendors, its wonderous palaces, temples, pavilions, gardens, and its profound serenity, *Peking* is rightfully renamed *Peiping*, which means "Northern Peace."

Each year, as summer deepens into autumn, the walled city of *Peiping* becomes arid, and gusts of wind carry whirls of dust until the city is covered by a thick carpet of silky velvetness. From this characteristic occurrence is derived the name for the following delicious dessert.

Peiping Dust Base

1 egg white	*½ tsp. vanilla*
¼ cup sugar	*⅛ tsp. cream of tartar*
	1 pinch of salt

Beat egg white and cream of tartar until stiff but not dry. Add salt and sugar a little at a time. Beat stiff after each addition. Fold in vanilla. Put mass into pastry bag and press out upon baking sheet covered with heavy ungreased paper. Bake egg white in slow oven (275°) about 40 to 60 minutes. Egg white should acquire a golden hue. Remove from paper at once, and when cool, cover with chestnut mixture.

Peiping Dust Filling

2 lbs. chestnuts	Milk
⅓ pint whipping cream	Maraschino cherries
⅛ pound butter	Brandy or rum
1 cup powdered sugar	Vanilla essence

Shell chestnuts and place in cold water. Boil 3 minutes and blanch. Place blanched chestnuts in pan, cover with milk, add a little vanilla essence, and simmer chestnuts until tender. Drain chestnuts and mash through strainer. Work in butter and powdered sugar to taste. Add brandy or rum to taste. If mass is extremely stiff, add a little cream. The consistency of the mass should be that of velvety mashed potatoes. Fill pastry bag with chestnut mash and press through small opening so that filling oozes out like vermicelli; or, place mass in sieve and press filling through holes so that threads of chestnut filling fall upon the meringue base.

Then whip remaining cream until stiff, sweeten with powdered sugar to taste and cover mound of chestnut dust generously. Garnish with maraschino cherries and serve.

Chapter XI

CHINESE TEA

THE most precious tree or shrub in China is that of the tea plant. Since the sixth century A. D., tea drinking has become more and more popularized in China. One of the blessings of the tea shrub is that it seems to prefer the poorer soil. The plant achieves a height of about three to five feet and produces glossy dark green leaves and waxy white blossoms. After the third year, the leaves may be plucked. The plant provides three pickings of leaves a year, but the first, which is ready in April, is the finest. Also, the higher the leaves are upon the shrub, the finer they are; and all leaves must be plucked within three to five days or else the tender leaves are spoiled for first quality production. From these leaves, two main types of tea, the green 青 *Chang* and the red (known abroad as "black tea") 紅 *Hoong*, are produced as a result of varying techniques in curing.

Te firing of tea leaves produces an aroma so fragrant that it floats and permeates everything for wide areas around. The favorite method for firing tea leaves is to set them out upon flat trays in rooms of graduating temperature to wither or steam. After they have withered sufficiently, they are then curled and twisted by hand. The leaves are then dried and packed in loose form or in brick form. Tea bricks are generally made out of tea-leaf dust. This

179

dust is steamed and then put into molds and compressed by hydraulic pressure. Most medicinal and powerful teas are sold in this form. Chinese tea is on the whole much less astringent than Indian or other teas. It also possesses a much more pure and delicate flavor and fragrance. This delicacy of flavor and fragrance is often further enhanced by the addition of fragrant blossoms or fruit, like the Jasmin tea 茉莉花茶 *Mook Lay Faah Chaah* and the Lei-chee tea 荔枝茶 *Luy Jee Chaah*.

Below, I shall very briefly give you a shadow of a knowledge of some Chinese teas: From the Province of Kwangtung 廣東 one finds such gems as *Sûy Sien Chaah* 水仙茶 Water Nymph Tea (green); *Sao May Chaah* 壽眉茶 Eyebrows of Longevity Tea (green); *Ooloong Chaah* 烏龍茶 Black Dragon Tea (blackish red); *Loong So Chaah* 龍鬚茶 Dragon's Beard Tea (green); *Ngun Jum Chaah* 銀針茶 Silver Needles Tea (green); and *Ching Yuen Chaah* (name derived from place of origin) 清遠茶 Clear Distance Tea (red).

From the Province of Kiangsi 江西 one finds a delectable tea called *Wun Mo Chaah* 雲霧茶 Cloud Mist Tea (green). This tea is grown upon the very highest of mountain peaks at such an altitude that men seldom climb so high. Thus monkeys are trained to pluck the delicate leaves and to fill their baskets with them in order to bring them down to man.

From the Province of Yünnan 雲南 comes a powerful tonic reddish-black tea called *Po Nay Chaah* 普洱茶, and from the Province of Szechwan 四川 another powerful brick tea called *Taw Chaah* 沱茶 may be obtained. From the Province of Fukien 福建 come two jewels, both red teas: *Teet Gwoon Yum Chaah* 鐵觀音茶 Iron Goddess of Mercy Tea; and *Mo Yee Chaah* (name derived from place of origin) 武夷茶. And, from the Province of Chinkiang 浙江 one may obtain two green teas of pure deliciousness of fragrance and flavor. They are *Loong Jang Chaah* (name derived from place of origin) 龍井茶 Dragon's

Well Tea (green) and *Heung Pien Chaah* 香片茶 Fragrant Petals Tea (green).

Tea is such a necessary refreshment in China that it is served all day long in homes, offices, and tea-houses. In China, the tea-house is a place of refreshment as well as amusement and information. People gather there all day long to exchange the latest news or gossip.

Tea is generally steeped in two ways; in a porcelain teapot, or in individual lidded cups. To steep tea in a porcelain teapot is by far the simplest and most economical method when there are many people. The interior of the pot is first scalded with boiling water, then the leaves are tossed in, about ½ to 1 teaspoon for each measuring cup of water. The boiling water is then poured into the pot, the lid is placed securely on, and the tea is left to steep for a few moments before serving. To make tea in individual cups, a generous ½ teaspoon of leaves is placed in the bottom of each cup, boiling water is poured over the leaves, the lid is placed upon the cup, and a few moments are given for the tea to steep. To drink tea from a lidded cup, the cup is daintily held in the hand and the forefinger is used to push back the lid sufficiently to allow the tea to flow when the cup is tipped.

After one finishes the tea in either teapot or cups, one should not throw away the residue of saturated leaves, because much pure flavor may be obtained from the leaves with a second or even third steeping of boiling water, since, with all good quality tea leaves, most of the pure delicate flavors and fragrances manifest themselves with the second steeping.

To store the tea, keep the leaves in a tight-lidded can in a cool dry place. Tea leaves possess volatile oils which are responsible for much of their fragrance and flavor. These evaporate easily. Tea leaves also have a marked tendency to absorb moisture and unwanted odors.

Chapter XII

CHINESE FESTIVAL DISHES

New Year

FIRST in importance among Chinese Festivals is the celebration of *Sun Neen* 新 年 Chinese New Year, which begins one week before the old year ends, and when the God of the Kitchen 竈 君 ascends to heaven to report to *Sheung Duy* 上 帝 Almighty God, all the virtues and vices of each member of the family. So, on the twenty-third day of the Twelfth Moon the family gathers before the picture of the Kitchen God which is pasted upon the kitchen chimney of every home. Accompanied by the sound of noisy popping of firecrackers, which are supposed to chase the evil spirits away, the family worships him and then smears his lips with molasses and other sticky sweets. This is to induce him to speak nothing but good, or to seal his lips so thoroughly that he will not be able to utter anything evil. Then the picture is taken down, placed upon a chariot or horse made of reeds and paper, and

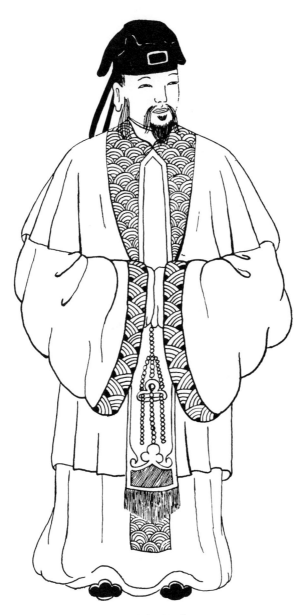

God of the Kitchen

brought to the principal courtyard with great ceremony. With even greater ceremony the Kitchen God upon his horse or chariot is burned, and in this way he rises swiftly along his spiritual way to heaven.

On the thirtieth day of the Twelfth Moon the family gathers around the kitchen furnace once more; this time to welcome the return of the God of the Kitchen with displays of delicious food and the cheerful sound of firecrackers. The new and gaudy picture of the Kitchen God is pasted upon the chimney, and prayers are offered to encourage his generosity and good will during the New Year.

This period of celebration reaps a world of good, for it promotes benevolence and reunions. People in their best finery pay their respects to parents, grandparents, friends, acquaintances, and deceased ancestors. Kindnesses are shown to one and all, and petty quarrels are patched up. Also, before the breaking of dawn of the New Year, all debts are settled. This is to insure the saving of the face of the borrower, and to bring good fortune to him and his family all during the coming year.

煎 堆

Jien Dûy

½ lb. glutinous rice powder	⅔ cup boiling water
(naw muy fun)	½ cup snow white sesame seeds
½ cup brown sugar	(jieh maah)
½ lb. dow saah (black bean filling)	

Dissolve brown sugar in water and bring to swift boil. Take sugar water off fire and carefully stir into glutinous rice powder until a well-blended dough is formed. Roll dough into sausage about 1 inch in diameter, then cut off 1-inch sections (makes about 20). Roll each section into ball with palms of hands.

Roll the *Dow Saah* filling into sausage about ½ inch in diameter. Cut off sections ½-inch wide. Roll each piece into ball.

Take ball of dough and flatten it in hand. Place ball of filling upon it and envelop filling with dough completely. Roll ball of filled dough until smooth in the palms of hands, and dip ball in snow white sesame seeds until entire surface is covered. Gently press seeds into surface. Place ball gently in 3 inches of hot fat and fry at least 10 minutes, until cooked through and until surface acquires attractive orange-gold hue. Serve hot. Care must be taken not to eat too many *jien dûy*. The temptation is great after one has had one or two . . . one is always tempted to eat one too many, or rather, ten too many.

The Lantern Festival

The Lantern Festival falls on the fifteenth day of the First Moon, but festivities extend from the thirteenth to the sixteenth day of the month. *Dung-Loong Jeet* 燈 龍 節 Lantern Festival dates back over two thousand years to the Han Dynasty. It was a ceremonial worship celebrating the return of light, spring, and the

The Lantern Festival

lengthening of day. In all parts of town in China, great poles are erected, and from the top of these are strung long strands of lanterns. The ends of these strings are attached to the ground, and the final effect resembles that of a brilliantly glittering tentlike Maypole. Processions are arranged too; and, wearing colorful costumes and masks, the boys and peasants carry exquisite lanterns made in every conceivable shape, size, and color. Some lanterns represent animals, some mythical creatures, and others geometric

186

designs. The entire effect is a combination of a Roman Festival and Macy's Thanksgiving Parade. The peak of hilarity is reached upon the breath-taking sight of the dance of the parading dragon. This gigantic mythical creature is made of bamboo framework covered by silk or paper. He is often over a hundred feet long and is shouldered and supported by men who expose only their legs. The creature is then carried dancing merrily and careening recklessly as it wends it tortuous way through noisy throngs of loudly cheering people. With the end of the Lantern Festival, all New Year festivities are officially at a close.

Tong Yuen   Soup Globes

½ lb. sago
1 cup glutinous rice powder
   (naw muy fun)
1 cup brown sugar

½ lb. dow saah (black bean
   filling)
1 large piece ginger
1½ qts. of water

Soak sago 3 to 4 hours, drain for ½ hour, and then knead and press grains until fine. Knead in 1 cup of *naw muy fun*. When dough is well blended, take up a bit of dough and roll in palms of hands into a ball about the size of a large cherry.

Roll *dow saah* filling into a sausage about ½ inch in diameter, and cut off sections ¼-inch wide. Roll each disk into ball the size of a tiny cherry.

Take ball of dough, flatten in your palm, and place tiny ball of filling in center. Bring edges of dough up and fully envelop filling. Weld all seams securely by carefully pressing seams together and then rolling filled ball gently with palms of hands. If ball has slightest imperfection in welding, it will be unsuccessful as a globe.

If hands become sticky and gluey during process of making these balls, wash them frequently under cold tap, and dry them thoroughly before starting work on the rest of the dough.

In the meanwhile, crush brown sugar, and boil in 1½ quarts water with large piece of sliced ginger. When all balls are ready, turn sweet soup down to gentlest of simmers, drop in balls carefully, and continue cooking until balls float to surface. When balls float, it means that they are cooked and almost ready. Simmer 10 minutes longer and serve hot.

Festival of the Flowers

The Chinese are skilled and proud horticulturists possessing extraordinary devotion to blossoms and flowers. Each flower represents an appropriate symbol; and it is believed that when each woman enters the heavenly world, a flower which she most resembles in spirit, character, and appearance springs to life and blossoms on earth. On the twelfth day of the Second Moon, when the mellowest day of spring dawns, and when all the plants adorn their coats of jade, a beautiful festival, *Faah Jiu* 花朝 Flower Dawn takes place in honor of *Faah Seen* 花仙 the Taoist Goddess of Flowers. Women and children begin the day by first suspending brightly colored silk and paper blooms upon the trees and shrubberies; then, bedecked in elaborate finery and flowers, they gather to pray for a season of fruitfulness. The headdresses of the married women are most exquisite and graceful. If they are ·not ornamented with artificial blossoms, then real flowers are used and kept fresh and lovely in a tube of water, which is then very carefully inserted in the intricate headdress.

During the festival, the delicacy of the occasion is *tung law bang* 藤蘿餅 rattan flower cake. Only rattan flowers, Kraunhia floribunda, may be used in this unleavened, strained suet and flour flat cake of a porous nature and agreeable flavor. The blossoms of the rattan flower are exquisitely butterfly shaped and of either a purple or white color.

Faah Seen, Goddess of the Flowers

Ching Ming

On the third day of the Third Moon, or exactly one hundred and six days after the winter solstice, *Ching Ming* 清明 the Festival of the Tombs is celebrated. It is a time when all the Chinese visit the graves of their ancestors, put them in order, and present food and other offerings to the departed.

The Chinese believe that the world of spirits is likened to the world of men, and that souls cannot possibly rest in peace and ease unless they also possess the comforts of earthly men. So, paper images of all necessary comforts, such as money, homes, servants, carriages, horses, and clothes are burned and pass into the invisible world through the form of smoke.

Filial piety, which is a great asset of any people, is preserved strongly in China through Ancestral Worship and respect. For three days prior to *Ching Ming*, no fires may be lit in the homes; and so, for this reason, this period is sometimes called the "Festival of the Cold Food." However, after the graves have been put in order, and proper honor has been given the ancestors, fires may be rekindled, and festivities may take place.

During *Ching Ming* families partake of a delicious nine-layer pudding called 九層糕, *Gow Chung Go*. Numbers in China usually possess some kind of significance, and certain numerical combinations are extremely felicitous: for example, the Three Plenties and the Nine Complimentaries 三多九如 *Saam Daw Gow Yü*. The Three Plenties are: sons, wealth, and longevity. The numeral "9" is related to sacred power and ever-flowing life. When the Altar of Heaven 天壇 *Tien Tan* was built in Peiping, it was constructed with amazing mathematical exactitude in multiples of nine. Most pagodas have nine tiers; and, symbolically also, there are nine species of dragons, each dragon possessing nine likenesses.

191

Comforts rising to the spirit world in the form of smoke

The Nine Complimentaries (or resemblances) were compiled in an ageless poem which Confucius found and added to his anthology, *The Book of Songs*, during the Chou Dynasty.

THE NINE COMPLIMENTARIES

Like unto mountains,
Like unto hills,
Like unto ridges,
Like unto mounds,
Like unto new sprung streams
    forever augmentingly flowing,
Like unto moon's steadfast rhythm,
Like unto sun's arising,
Like unto Naam Saan's longevity,
    ineffaceable, indestructible,
Like unto exuberant pine and cypress,
    harmonic green abounding
    ere is shed the old.

CHINESE ORIGINAL OF THE POEM

如 山

如 阜

如 岡

如 陵

如 川 之 方 至

如 月 之 恒

如 日 之 昇

如 南 山 之 壽

如 松 栢 之 茂

九層糕

Gow Chung Go   Nine-Layer Pudding

1 lb. pure rice flour	¼ cup vegetable oil
½ lb. brown sugar	¼ cup snow white sesame seeds
¼ cup white sugar	4 cups water

Boil 2 cups water and add brown sugar. Boil syrup 5 minutes and then strain into clean bowl to cool. Pour pure rice flour into mixing bowl, and when syrup is cool, add slowly to rice flour, stirring mixture constantly until well blended. Add 1 to 2 cups water slowly while stirring until a medium thin batter is achieved. Beat in vegetable oil and white sugar.

Prepare about 4 inches boiling water in large steamer. Grease deep pie dish (8 or 9 inches in diameter) generously with oil. When water in steamer is boiling, heat greased pan, beat batter smooth, pour ½ cup batter into pan (tip pan gently until batter covers entire surface evenly), cover steamer with lid, and steam first layer 4 minutes. Then stir up batter, pour another half cup evenly over first layer. Cover steamer with dried-off lid, and steam second and first layer another 3 to 4 minutes. Repeat process six times more. When it comes to the ninth layer, pour remaining batter upon eighth layer, fold dish cloth over mouth of steamer under lid to catch steam-drippings, and steam entire pudding 10 to 15 minutes.

In the meanwhile, toast snow white sesame seeds over low fire until of light golden hue. When pudding is done, sprinkle toasted seeds evenly over surface. Press in lightly. Loosen pudding from sides of pan, turn out upon a board to cool, and then turn right side up on serving dish. Serve cold.

Another way of eating this pudding which is even more delicious than eating it in its fresh state is to wait until the pudding is at least one day old, slice it into pieces about ¼-to ⅓-inch thick, covering each piece with batter of beaten eggs, a little cornstarch, and sugar, and frying these dipped pieces in 1 inch of hot fat until batter acquires rich golden-brown hue. Serve hot.

Race of the dragon boats

The Dragon Boat Festival

During the first five days of the Fifth Moon, *Loong Shün Jeet* 龍 船 節 Dragon Boat Festival is celebrated in honor of *Wut Yuen* 屈 原 a minister of the State of Ch'u during the Chou Dynasty. About 295 B. C., this virtuous statesman was wronged and falsely accused by a corrupt and scheming prince. *Wut Yuen,* in protest against the foul government, tied a stone to his body and drowned himself in the River *Gwut Lowe* 汩 羅. The people, who loved him dearly for his uprightness and goodness, hurriedly set out in their boats to search for his body. But the search was in vain, and in order to compensate for their failure, they prepared a kind of food called *Joong* 糭 a glutinous rice pudding wrapped in leaves, and sent these down to the bottom of the river to him. However, *Wut Yuen* appeared in a dream to make it known that he was unable to eat any *Joong* these kind people gave him because the dragons of the river liked them so well that they ate them all up. He requested these faithful friends to tie the *Joong* with brightly colored straw since the dragons were timorous of color and noise. So from then on, the friends of *Wut Yuen* began using colored straws and ribbons, and also commenced building larger, fleeter crafts in the form of fierce dragons. In these, the people would race each other to the scene of disaster accompanied by the exciting sound of clanging gongs and the sight of bright, waving banners. Nowadays, the race of the dragon boats is still held, but the boats have become increasingly large and elaborate. Some are as long as 125 feet. The boats are usually five and a half feet in width and two and a half feet in depth. The head of the dragon ornaments the bow, and the tail of the dragon naturally decorates the stern. The waving of the flags is supposed to excite the oarsmen to greater exertion, and the beating of gongs and other percussions is to drive away all evil spirits.

197

鹹 糭

Haahm Joong   Salty Joong

1 lb. naw muy (glutinous rice)	½ lb. chaah sieu (roast pork)
1 cup lien jee (lotus seeds)	10 Chinese mushrooms
¼ cup baak haap (100 Unities)	2 tbls. oil
entirely optional	¼ tsp. soda
½ lb. dried green peas	4 dozen dried corn leaves and
¼ lb. slab of bacon	1-yard lengths of string

2 tsp. salt

Soak *naw muy* overnight in cold water. Drain at least ½ hour and mix with salt and oil. Cook *lien jee* in pot of cold water with a pinch of baking soda. Bring water to a boil. Scrub off as much of the brown husks as possible, then let *lien jee* soak in cold water until all husk floats off. Boil *baak haap* in water for 10 minutes and then add to pot of cold water in which *lien jee* are soaking. Cook the two together for about 20 minutes. Boil peas 15 minutes and take off the tough green skin around each pea. Finally fine-dice Chinese mushrooms that have soaked until soft, and plain-dice *chaah sieu* and bacon. Blend all prepared ingredients with rice mixture. Then prepare leaves and fill with above stuffing. Wrap as explained and illustrated (see page 199). This recipe will make one dozen *joong*.

How to Wrap Joong in Corn Leaves

4 dozen large dried white corn leaves. (The larger and more perfect the easier to handle.)

1 dozen pieces of white string or raffia at least 1½ yards long each

Wash leaves thoroughly with warm water and coarse salt. Drain leaves and cut off about an inch from base of each leaf with pair of shears or with whack of sharp blade of cleaver. Pile leaves neatly upon cleared surface of kitchen table. Then stretch lengths of white string or raffia neatly nearby. Then place bowl of ingredients on table within easy reach.

1) Flatten corn leaves upon the table with bases and inner sides overlapping about 3 inches. Use about 4 large leaves for each *joong*. Place about 3 heaping tablespoons mixed salty filling neatly upon overlapping portions of 4 leaves.

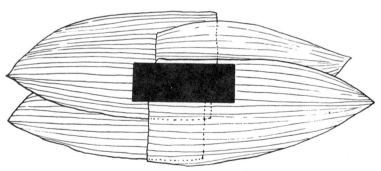

How to wrap *joong* — 1

Place filling upon overlapping portions of leaves

2) Bring sides of leaves carefully up and over so that edges overlap each other generously or at least by 1 inch. Stretch *joong* slightly until taut, and then fold ends by tucking them under body of *joong*.

199

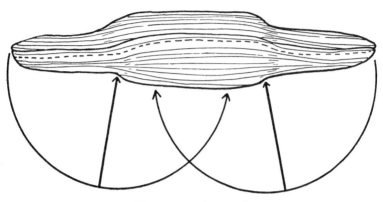

How to wrap *joong* — 2

Fold ends by tucking them under body of joong

3) Take a string and tie it securely around *joong*. Care must be taken to allow a slight leeway towards center of *joong*, for *joong* will expand during the cooking.

4) Drop each prepared *joong* into large pot of boiling water, and allow to simmer 10 hours. After they are cooked, place on serving dish and serve hot. Unwrap *joong* at table so that, in case any are left over, they may be reheated by steaming. Reheated *joong* taste much better than the original batch!

This is not the real method of wrapping *joong*, nor do the Chinese usually use white corn leaves. The Chinese use fragrant lotus leaves for wrapping up the filling, and these lose their fragrance in the *joong*. Lotus leaves are hard to obtain abroad, and the true method of folding and tying them is difficult. This substitute method of using corn leaves is comparatively easy and will at least insure water repellence during the long hours of gentle simmering. If water enters *joong*, the result can be awfully messy!

200

甜 糭

Tiem Joong   Sweet Joong

2 *lbs.* naw muy *(glutinous rice)*	1 *lb.* dow saah *filling (black bean*
1 *tbls. vegetable oil*	*filling)*
4 *doz. dried white corn leaves*	12 *strings* 1½ *yards long*

Soak the *naw muy* overnight in cold water. Drain for at least
½ hour. Mix rice with oil. Roll *dow saah* filling (sweet black bean
filling) into sausage about 1 inch in diameter. Cut off 3-inch
lengths, and flatten each slightly. Stretch out the white corn leaves
in the manner illustrated, place glutinous rice mixture upon overlapping area, place the piece of filling upon rice layer, and then
cover filling with generous layer of glutinous rice. After this wrap
joong as illustrated (see pages 199 and 200). Makes about 1 dozen
joong. Stew like Salty *Joong* for 10 hours.

The Herd Boy and the Weaver Maid

On the seventh day of the Seventh Moon is the festival of the Herd Boy and the Weaver Maid 牛郎織女 *Ngow Long Jick Nûy*. Ancient folklore has it that once upon a time the Sun God had a very beautiful daughter who confined herself so closely to her work that he feared she would miss happiness and decided to give her in marriage to a handsome herd boy. However, so great was the change wrought upon her character after this taste of happiness, and so lazy did she become, that the king and queen of heaven, in a fit of anger, decided to separate them. With a stroke of her silver hair-pin, the queen drew a line across the heavens and formed a silver stream or Milky Way. Then the Sun God ordered a flock of beautiful magpies to form a bridge across the heavenly stream and sent the poor herd boy far away to the other side of heaven. So, the herd boy and the weaver maid may be seen as stars on either side of the Milky Way under the names of Altair in the constellation Aquila, and Vega in Lyra. They are forbidden to meet except for one day each seven years; and so, on the seventh day of the Seventh Moon, when the compassionate magpies flock together again, they form a bridge over which the weaver maid may lightly run to meet her herd boy husband. If it rains, however, she will have to wait until the following seven years. For this reason, all the sympathetic maidens pray for fair weather on this day. They also offer her gifts of watermelon, luscious fruits, and sweetmeats; and in return they beg her for guidance in needle work and increased skill.

The favorite fruit eaten on this day is the famous Chinese *loong ngaan* 龍眼 dragons' eyes. This fruit is eaten by the maidens in the hope that their eyesight may improve in order to enable them to do finer weaving and embroidering. The girls also compete in making miniature homes, dolls, shoes, and clothing out of sesame

202

Herd Boy and Weaver Maid

seeds glued together. But the most important competition of all is that of the "Threading of the Needle" by moonlight. The maiden who is able to accomplish this feat first is the winner and star of the evening.

Loong ngaan — dragons' eyes

Watermelon Basket

During the seventh day of the Seventh Moon Festival, everyone indulges in fruits served both fresh, iced, or candied. Watermelons and dragons' eyes are favorites at this season. Seven fruits are generally served at one time. The following recipe is one for the ex-

204

quisite watermelon basket which is always such a picture of prettiness and succulent coolness upon any summer table.

1 medium-sized watermelon preferably round as possible	4 firm yellow peaches fresh or canned (8 halves)
1 cantaloupe or	1 cup sweet sherry
1 Persian melon	2 bunches grapes: 1 green and 1 red
2 oranges	
20 maraschino cherries	1 can dragons' eyes or 1 can litchi

Powdered sugar or honey

With sharp knife, carefully cut watermelon to form broad-handled basket (see illustration). Then with fruit ball spoon, make balls of firm red meat of watermelon and meat of either cantaloupe or Persian melon. Place balls in mixing bowl. Hollow out watermelon so that it is neat within.

How to prepare a watermelon basket

Peel each segment of orange and slice peaches into thin wedges. If the circular objects are eyes and full moons, then these wedge-shaped objects are smiling eyes and new moons. Place all fruits except grapes in mixing bowl. If the fruit is likely to be too juicy, place fruit in colander suspended in mixing bowl so that most of juice may drain through. Keep fruits in refrigerator until 1 hour before using. Place in watermelon basket, mix thoroughly with sweet sherry and powdered sugar or honey to taste. Wash grapes and hang upon handle. Tie with an enormous bow that will match the table decorations. If bunches of grapes are too big or straggly, pluck off stray grapes and mix with rest of fruit.

All Souls' Day

All Souls' Day 盂蘭盆會 *Yü Laahn Poon Wuy*, on the fifteenth of the Seventh Moon, is a wonderfully compassionate Buddhist festival in honor of the unhappy dead or "orphaned spirits" of those who passed over far from home, drowned, or have no descendants to perpetuate their memory through ancestral worship. During the festival, a deep-toned bell is struck every minute by a wooden beam, and gives forth a tone of melodious mellowness which is said to relieve the tormented souls of their pain. Offerings of useful gifts to ease their spiritual existence are presented in the form of paper images of servants, horses, money, homes, and garments. These images are burned and wafted heavenwards to them in the form of smoke.

Large numbers of people also make pilgrimages to the festival at the Monastary of *Ch'ing Leung Saahn* 清涼山 (Clear Cool Mountain) within the walled city of Nanking, which is dedicated to *Dey Jong Wong* 地藏王 the God of Hades. As the worshiper enters the temple, he first honors and prays to the gentle god; then, facing the altar, he picks up a vase of sortilage sticks, makes a wish, and carefully shakes the vase until one of the sticks falls out. This stick is then brought to the monks, who are able to give him the answer and advice of the god.

The festival lasts until the thirtieth of the Seventh Moon. On this day, the dead are believed to take a holiday, and great happiness is felt by all at the thought of the "orphaned spirits" enjoying release from the sorrows of lonesome death.

Dey Jong Wong — Gentle God of Hades

什錦齋菜

Sup Gum (Jaai Choy)   Vegetarian Dish

1 cup dried bamboo shoots	2 garlic cloves
8 Chinese mushrooms	½ cup faat choy (hairlike seaweed)
¼ cup cloud ears (wun yee)	1 handful fun see (cellophane noo-
¼ cup golden needles (gum jum)	dles)
2 squash or vegetable marrow	¼ lb. bean sprouts
6 pieces dried bean curd sheets	2 tbls. soya sauce
(tiem jook)	3 tbls. naam yü sauce
½ lb. slice of winter melon	1 tsp. sugar
1 tsp. salt	2 tbls. sherry (dry)

1 tsp. mei-jing (gourmet powder)

Soak dried bamboo shoots overnight in cold water. Soak Chinese mushrooms, cloud ears, golden needles, and *tiem jook* in warm water for 15 minutes. In separate bowl, soak *faat choy* for 1 hour. Cut bamboo into 2-inch lengths, smash the cloves of garlic, cut the *tiem jook* into squared or oblong pieces, and ·slice vegetable marrow coarsely diagonally. Slice winter melon into pieces 1 inch by 1 inch by ½ inch, heat a little oil in a pot, sprinkle melon cubes with salt and fry 3 minutes. Add vegetable marrow and fry another 3 minutes. Then add mushrooms, cloud ears, golden needles, bamboo, *tiem jook,* and garlic. Pour in 1 cup water in which mushrooms, and so on are soaked. Then add sauce made of *naam yü* sauce, soya sauce, and ¼ cup water. Stir into cooking vegetables and then add enough boiling water to cover vegetables. Cover pot with lid and simmer contents gently, stirring at intervals.

After the *faat choy* has soaked 1 hour, squeeze fresh water through mass until water comes out clear. Then pour 2 tablespoons oil upon the *faat choy,* place mass in colander and using whole hands squeeze oil into seaweed as if you were washing a pair of

209

thick stockings in sudsy water. When oil is thoroughly squeezed in, rinse seaweed in cold water until water runs through clear, and drain thoroughly. Then pour about 2 tablespoons cheap cooking sherry into seaweed and repeat process of squeezing seaweed and rinsing in cold water afterward. By this time the strands of *faat choy* should be clean and glistening. Add 2 tablespoons good dry sherry to mass and then add to simmering vegetables. Pour more boiling water into pot so that water level again reaches that of vegetables.

De-root and un-jacket bean sprouts (not pea sprouts). Fry with a little salt in a little heated oil for 2 minutes. Then add to simmering vegetables. Soak *fun see,* and after they are spread add to pot during last ½ hour of cooking time. Add *mei-jing* gourmet powder just before serving.

From the beginning to the end, vegetables simmer about 1½ hours. Cook in a large quantity, for this dish may be reheated several times with marked improvement to the taste each time.

If *tiem jook* is not available, use fresh bean curd cakes. The bean curd should be cut into pieces 1 inch by 1 inch by ½ inch and fried in hot deep fat until a golden crust is acquired. Add this fried bean curd *(dow fooh)* to the simmering vegetables at the same time as the *fun see.*

Festival of the Moon

The moon is the Queen of Heaven; and, on the fifteenth day of the Eighth Moon, when she gracefully rises full and at her brightest immediately after sunset, great celebrations take place in her honor. During the gay festivities and happy picnics given under the light of the harvest moon, refreshments, sweets, and round moon cakes, garnished sometimes with the shapes of pagodas, rabbits, and frogs, are served.

Many ancient legends present varying tales regarding the habitant of this serene heavenly abode. Some say that a rabbit sitting under the shade of a Cassia tree spends his time pounding and grinding the ingredients of gold, jade, and cinnebar into what goes to make up the Precious Elixir of Immortality. Others say that once upon a time, around 2500 B.C., a fairy queen of the West, *Suy Wong Mo* 西王母, gave the Elixir of Immortality to a handsome chieftain by the name of *Hao Ieh* 后羿. His exquisite wife, 嫦娥 *Sheung Aw,* however, stole it and drank it; and, in order to escape her husband's ire, fled to the moon for safety. Once here, the merciful gods of the heaven took pity and changed her into a three-legged toad, the symbol of unattainability. During "*Moon Yüt*" 滿月 as the Chinese call this festival, it is said that her outline may be traced at its very best upon the surface of the cool silvery luminary.

Around the fifteenth of the Eighth Moon, sweet shops, caterers, and restaurants are filled with little moon cakes. Moon cakes are seldom made at home, for the genuine type are difficult to make and require a long list of hard-to-prepare ingredients as well as special wooden forms and cooking implements.

Another specialty eaten on this festival, however, is *Woo Tao Ngaap* 芋頭鴨, Yams Braised With Duck, and the following recipe will describe to you the simple method of making it.

Sheung Aw seeking refuge in the moon

芋頭鴨

Woo Tao Ngaap   Yams Braised With Duck

1 *tender young 5½–6 months old*	¼ *cup dry sherry*
duck	2 *tbls. soya sauce*
4 *tbls.* naam yü *sauce*	1 *small piece ginger*
1 *tsp. sugar*	2 *scallions*
1 *tsp. salt*	2 *cloves garlic*
½ *tsp.* heung new fun *spices*	1 *lb. yams or potatoes*

Dress duck, sew up opening and then blow air into hole made in neck of duck (see illustration page 128). The air should fill up the area between duck and its skin, and after this performance, skin should be puffed, taut, and extremely smooth. Tie string around neck below hole in neck to prevent air from escaping rapidly.

Mix *naam yü* sauce, sugar, salt, *heung new fun* spices, and sherry. Take half of this mixture and rub all over inside of duck. Sew up duck again, wash off outer skin, and rub thoroughly with soya sauce. Heat about ⅛ inch of vegetable oil in a large pot. Fry ginger cut into thick slices and crushed once with flat of blade of knife, garlic, and scallions. Brown duck all over. Take out ginger, garlic, and scallions and then add to remaining half of *naam yü* sauce, to which 1 cup of boiling water has been added.

When duck is browned to an autumn leaf sienna with tinges of gold, red, and brown turn duck upon its back, add sauce mixture, and then enough boiling water to reach three fourths the height of duck. Simmer very, very gently on low fire about 2 hours.

In the meanwhile, peel 1 pound yams or potatoes. Cut into eighths and fry in deep hot fat until they acquire golden-brown crust. When duck is tender, take out duck, cook potatoes or yams in gravy and simmer until cooked. Return duck and cook everything until duck is reheated. Serve.

The Kite Flying Festival

The Kite Flying Festival

There is an ancient folk tale that relates that about one thousand years ago, during the Han Dynasty, there lived a wise and powerful magician by the name of *Fûy Cheung Fong* 費 長 房 who had a favorite pupil called *Woon Ging* 桓 景. On the ninth day of the Ninth Moon, *Fûy Cheung Fong* suddenly warned *Woon Ging* that great disaster would overtake the district wherein he lived, and that he should escape with his family and immediately flee to the highest mountain top. *Woon Ging*, although in a state of great anxiety and impatience, thoughtfully remembered to warn the rest of the community, but to no avail. So, he and his family fled alone; and, once upon the mountain top, fulfilled a series of duties to ward off evil. Everyone followed the precautions taught by the venerable magician, and wore tiny sacks containing dogwood fragments, and drank of wine in which floated chrysanthemum petals. After this, in order to while away the leisure time, *Woon Ging* amused his family and himself by making and flying fancy kites. In the meanwhile, terrible disasters and calamities did befall the community, and everyone there passed over into the land of spirits. So, today, upon each ninth day of the Ninth Moon, innumerable people betake themselves to the mountain tops to commemorate the happy fate of kindly *Woon Ging*. Now again, as before, they repeat the precautions of bedecking themselves with dogwood fragments, and of sipping wine in which lie soaking the fragrant petals of chrysanthemum. And, for amusement, boys and men vie with one another in the art of creating and flying kites, which are handsomely wrought in every imaginable color and design.

215

荷葉飯

Haw Yeep Faahn   Lotus Leaf Rice

3 *cups raw rice*
½ *lb.* chaah sieu *(roast pork)*
2 laap cheung *(Chinese sausages)*
1 *strip* laap yook *(dried pork)*
¼ *cup* laap ngaap *(dried duck)*
6 *dried scallops* (gon yiu chee)
1 *cup roasted peanuts*
6 *water chestnuts*
1 *cup bamboo shoots*

2 *scallions chopped*
6 doong gwooh *(Chinese mushrooms)*
¼ *cup soya sauce*
¼ *cup salad oil*
2 *tsp. salt*
2 *cups parsley leaves*
1 *doz. white strings or raffia 1½ yards long each*
4 *doz. dried white corn leaves*

Simmer dried scallops in 1 pint boiling water about 20 minutes. Take out scallops and shred. Soak mushrooms in scallop water. Dice water chestnuts, bamboo shoots, roast pork, Chinese sausage, dried salt pork, dried salt duck (remove all the bones). Chop scallions and slice mushrooms. Mix all ingredients together. Wash rice and pour grains into large pot. Add scallop water in which mushrooms soaked. Add 1 quart boiling water, 1 teaspoon vegetable oil, and 2 teaspoons salt. When water reaches boil again, allow rice to boil about 10 minutes and then add mixed ingredients. Mix thoroughly with rice. When rice is done, mix in crushed roasted peanuts, soya sauce, vegetable oil (sesame seed oil if available), and parsley leaves. Place generous helping of rice mixture upon each lotus leaf or 4 corn leaves and wrap packages in the manner described in the recipe for *Salty Joong* (see page 199). *Haw Yeep Faahn* need not be tied as securely as *joong* though, for the packages are merely steamed and not submerged under water. Steam packages about ½ hour before serving. *Haw Yeep Faahn* may be eaten hot or cold, but taste better hot. When wrapped in lotus leaves the rice absorbs a richly fragrant odor.

The Three Plenties

Festival of the Winter Solstice

Since ghosts are much more active in the dark, the Chinese believe that the spirit world is in the land of northern gloom. When the Eleventh Moon approaches with its winter chill and darkness, families prepare for the visit of their ancestors; a visit which is made on the longest night of the Winter Solstice. The ceremony of joyful reunion 冬 節 *Doong Jiet* is not held at the graves, however, but right in the ancestral temple or principal hall of the home. Here all the living members of the family gather together for the feast in honor of their visiting ancestors. A table is placed before the family altar, and is heavily laden with delicacies. Seats and dishes are placed for the visitors at the northern end of the table, and the living members sit facing them. After very reverently giving them honor, the head of the house motions to the spiritual guests to partake of the feast; then, after a few respectful moments of waiting for them to indulge in the ethereal portion of the meal, the living members are invited to partake of the rich feast of fragrantly steaming viands, especially White Turnips Pudding.

During the Winter Solstice, the sight of orange-gold tangerines brightens homes and dining tables, and their heavy tangy scent permeates the air. Everyone at this time indulges in the presenting of gifts of even numbers of tangerines to those upon whom they wish the blessings of good luck; for, in China, tangerines are called *gut* 橘 and this word is phonetically similar to the word meaning "good luck."

蘿蔔糕

Law Baak Go White Turnip Pudding

2½ lbs. white long turnips
1 lb. pure rice flour
6 scallions
¼ cup laam gok (Chinese dried olives)
4 slices bacon
6 Chinese shrimps (haah muy)

6 Chinese mushrooms
1 cup parsley leaves
¼ cup vegetable oil
1 tsp. salt
½ tsp. pepper
½ tsp. mei-jing (gourmet powder)
3 cups turnip water

Peel white turnips and simmer in 1 quart boiling water about 2 hours, until extremely tender. Mince with cleaver, and place mass in large mixing bowl. Blend rice flour in and slowly stir in 3 cups turnip water.

Chop scallions, olives, bacon, soaked shrimps, and Chinese mushrooms. Add all these ingredients and parsley leaves to turnip mixture. Mix in oil, salt, pepper, and mei-jing gourmet powder. Blend all ingredients thoroughly.

Grease large pie dish or cake pan. Pour batter into it and steam for 2 hours. When pudding shrinks from edge of pan, it is done. Allow pudding to cool, turn out upon dish and place in the refrigerator to chill overnight. To serve, cut off generous slices from pudding, fry slices until golden crust is formed all around. Serve hot. Pudding may be eaten fresh, too, without frying.

Index of Recipes

abalone *(bow yü)*, 31, 32
Appetizers, 56–73:
  cloud swallows *(wun tun)*, 65
    filling, chicken, 68
    fried *(jaah wun tun)*, 69
    velvet chicken broth *(ghuy tong wun tun)*, 69
  flaky pastry *(sou gock)*, 56
    salty filling *(haahm sou gock sum)*, 60
    sweet bean filled *(dow saah gock)*, 60
  spring roll No. 1 *(chün gün No. 1)*, 70
    No. 2 *(chün gün No. 2)*, 71
    filling No. 1, 71
    filling No. 2, 73
  transparent dumplings *(gow jee)*, 61
    fried *(jaah gow jee)*, 63
    stuffed salty *(haahm sum gow jee)*, 64
    sweet bean filled *(dow saah gow jee)*, 64

baak-choy (Chinese cabbage), 24
baak choy tong (Chinese cabbage soup), 74
baak faahn (white rice), 162
baak faahn yü (white upside down fish), 101
baak gup (pigeon), 111
baak haap (one hundred unities), 29, 30
baak jaahm ghuy (white cut chicken), 117
baat bo faahn (eight-treasure rice), 173
bamboo shoots *(jook sün)*, 31, 32
baw law ghuy (pineapple chicken) 121
baw law ngaap (pineapple duck), 129

bean-sprouts *(dow ngaah)*, 21,23
beef, hundred abdomen of *(ngow baak naam)*, 20, 36, 37
bitter melon (balsam pear—*fooh gwaah*), 26
bow yü (abalone), 31, 32
bow yü tong (abalone soup), 78

cabbage, Chinese *(baak choy)*, 24
cabbage, pickled *(haahm choy, choong choy, mooi choy)*, 26, 27
chaah gwaah (tea melon), 27
chaah gwaah jing jüh yook (tea melons steamed with pork), 153
chaah sieu (barbecued pork), 136
cheung sao mien (long life noodles), 166
chicken *(ghuy)*, 110, 111
ching jew chow ghuy pien (bell pepper braised chicken), 118
ching jing baak gup (steamed velvet squab), 122
ching-jing doong gwooh (clear steamed Chinese mushrooms), 103
ching tong yü to (clear broth fish tripe), 85
choong (onions), 23, 24
choong choy (pickled cabbage), 26
chop sticks *(faai jee)*, 50–52
chop suey, 12
chow bow yü pien (braised abalone), 104
chow faahn No. 1 and No. 2 (fried rice No. 1 and No. 2), 163
chow haah look (fried shrimp curls), 106
chow yook soong (fried tasty meat mince), 154
chow yü (braised fish), 100
chúy mow faah (crisp *mow* flowers), 176
cloud ears *(wun yee)*, 27
cloud swallows *(wun tun)*, 65

daahn faah (egg garnish), 92

dates, Chinese red *(hoong joe)*, 28

deem sum (appetizers), 35, 49, 56–73

Desserts, 169–178:
  almond lake, mock *(hung yun woo)*, 174
  almond tea, genuine *(hung yun chaah)*, 174
  crisp *mow* flowers *(chûy mow faah)*, 176
  eight-treasure rice *(baat bo faahn)*, 173
  jien dûy, 184
  nine-layer pudding *(gow chung go)*, 194
  Peiping dust, 177
    base, 177
    filling, 178
  sesame seed cake *(jieh maah baang)*, 175
  soup globes *(tong yuen)*, 187
  sponge cake, Chinese *(ghuy daahn go)*, 175
  watermelon basket, 204
  white turnip pudding *(law baak go)*, 219

doong gwaah joong (winter melon pond), 82

doong gwooh (Chinese mushrooms), 27

dow chow jüh yook (lima beans braised with pork), 150

dow gock chow jüh yook (cow peas braised with pork), 157

dow ngaah (bean sprouts), 21, 23

dow saah gock (sweet bean filled pastry), 60

dow saah gow jee (sweet bean filled dumplings), 64

dow see (fermented beans), 32

dow see loong haah (Cantonese lobster), 109

duck *(ngaap)*, 110, 111

dun baak gup (broth of pigeon), 81

Egg dishes, 87–93
  egg garnish *(daahn faah)*, 92
  omelet, rich *(foo yoong daahn)*, 90
  pouch omelet *(ghuy daahn gow)*, 91
  steamed custard *(jing daahn)*, 89

eggs, ancient *(pay daahn)*, 93
  scrambled, with peas, *(woon dow chow daahn)*, 91
  cellophane noodle *(fun see jüh yook daahn)*, 88
  coin purse *(haw bow)*, 89

Eight Treasures, the, 169–172

essence of flavor *(mei jing)*, 35

faahn gwaah (vegetable marrow, Chinese squash), 26

faahn gwaah chow ngow yook (squash braised with beef), 155

faahn keh chow ngow yook (tomato braised with beef), 151

faai jee (chop sticks), 50–52

faat choy (hair vegetable), 135

fish *(yü)*, 96

Fish and Shellfish, 94–109:
  chicken-fat braised carp *(ghuy yow lay yü)*, 99
  fish, braised *(chow yü)*, 100
    tripe *(yü to)*, 84
  five-willows *(ngung lao yü)* 97
  mince, how to prepare, 101, 102
  steamed *(jing yü)*, 100
  stuffed *(yeung yü)*, 98
    bitter melon *(yü yeung fooh gwaah)* 103
    braised squash *(yeung gwaah* 102
    clear steamed Chinese mushrooms *(ching jing doong gwooh)*, 103
  sweet sour pungent *(tiem shün yü)*, 97
  white upside down *(baak faahn yü)*, 101

abalone, braised (*chow bow yü pien*), 104

    oyster sauce braised (*ho yow bow yü pien*), 105

lobster, Cantonese (*dow see long haah*), 109

shrimp balls, tomato braised (*keh jup chow haah kow*), 107

    Yang Chow (*Yang Chow haah kow*), 108

shrimp curls, fried (*chow haah look*), 106

shrimps, pea sprouts braised with (*ngaah choy chow haah*), 105

foo yoong daahn (rich egg omelet), 90

fooh gwaah (bitter melon), 26

fooh jook (soya bean), 30, 31

fooh yü (bean curd cheese), 32, 33

foong lüt ghuy (chicken chestnuts), 121

fun see jüh yook daahn (cellophane noodle eggs), 88

gaah heung ngaap (home-style duck), 124

gaah li ghuy (curried chicken), 119

gaah li ngow naam (curried beef plate), 144

gaai laan chow chaah sieu (broccoli braised with roast pork), 156

geung (fresh ginger root), 24, 25

ghuy daahn go (Chinese sponge cake), 175

ghuy daahn gow (egg pouch omelet), 91

ghuy gon tong (chicken liver soup), 76

ghuy tong wun tun (velvet chicken broth *wun tun*), 69

ghuy yoong low sün (melted asparagus soup), 81

ghuy yoong yien waw (swallow's nest soup), 85

ghuy yow lay yü (chicken-fat braised carp), 99

ging jeung ngaap (Peking sauce duck), 125

ginger root (*geung*), 24, 25

golden needles (*gum jum*), 28

gon yiu chee (dried scallops), 33

gow chung go (nine-layer pudding), 194

gow jee (transparent dumplings), 61

gum jum (golden needles), 28

gwaah jee choy tong (Chinese watercress soup), 77

haahm choy (pickled cabbage), 26

haahm joong (salty joong), 198

haahm sou gock sum (salty flaky pastry filling), 60

haahm sum gow jee (stuffed salty dumplings), 64

haap to ghuy (chicken walnuts), 119

haw bow daahn (coin purse eggs), 89

haw laahn dow (Chinese pea), 24

haw yeep faahn (lotus leaf rice), 216

heung new fun (spices of five fragrances, powdered), 33

ho see (dried Chinese oysters), 29

hoong joe (Chinese red dates), 28

hoong sieu jüh yook (casserole of five-flowered pork), 136

ho yow (oyster sauce), 32

ho yow bow yü pien (oyster sauce braised abalone), 105

ho yow dow fooh (oyster sauce bean curds), 155

hundred unities (*baak haap*), 29, 30

hung yun chaah (genuine almond tea), 174

hung yun woo (mock almond lake), 174

Ieh Fooh mien (*Ieh Fooh* noodles), 167

jaah baak gup (browned squab), 122

jaah gow jee (fried transparent dumplings), 63

jaah wun tun (fried wun tun), 69

jaak taai (bound trotters), 143

jee bow ghuy (paper-wrapped chicken), 113

jeung (Chinese sauces), 32, 33

jeung yow (soya sauce), 21, 32

jieh maah baang (sesame seed cakes), 175

jien dûy, 184

jing daahn (steamed egg custard), 89

jing loong (steam lantern), 37, 38

jing yü (steamed fish), 100

jook sün (bamboo shoots), 31, 32

jow jick (wine banquet), 44

jüh (pigs), 132

jüh gerk fooh jook tong (pig's feet soya bean soup), 80

jüh yook jook (pork congee), 164

jüh yow (strained pork suet), 35

jup (gravy), 17, 18

kay jee ghuy (chicken chessmen), 115

keh chow jüh yook (eggplant braised with pork), 159

keh jup chow haah kow (tomato braised shrimp balls), 107

laat jew jeung (chilied mince meat) 150

law baak chow ngow yook (turnips braised with beef), 153

law baak go (white turnip pudding), 219

lichi-nuts, 47

lien jee (lotus seeds), 29

lien ngow (lotus stem), 26

lien ngow tong (lotus root soup), 79

lotus (Chinese water lily), 147, 148

lotus seeds *(lien jee)*, 29

lotus stem *(lien ngow)*, 26

maah tuy (water chestnuts), 31, 32

maw gwooh (button mushrooms), 28

maw gwooh ghuy pien (mushrooms braised velvet chicken), 116

maw gwooh mun baak gup (casserole of mushroom squabs), 123

Meat Dishes, 130–144:

   beef plate, curried *(gaah li ngow naam)*, 144

   pig, roast *(sieu jüh)*, 134

   pig's feet, sweet-sour No. 1 *(tiem shün jüh gerk* No. 1), 139

   sweet-sour No. 2 *(tiem shün jüh gerk* No. 2), 140

   pork, barbecued *(chaah sieu)*, 136

   casserole of five-flowered *(hoong sieu jüh yook)*, 136

   round ham of *(yuen taai)*, 135

   spareribs, barbecued *(sieu pi gwut)*, 138

   sweet-sour *(tiem shün pi gwut)*, 138

   trotters, bound *(jaak taai)*, 143

   Yang Chow lion's head *(Yang Chow see jee tao)*, 141

mei jing (essence of flavor), 35

melon, bitter (balsam pear—*fooh gwaah)*, 26

melon, tea *(chaah gwaah)*, 27

mooi choy (pickled cabbage), 26, 27

mooi choy jing yook bang (pickled cabbage steamed with pork), 152

mushrooms, Chinese *(doong gwooh)*, 27, 28

naam yü (bean curd cheese), eastern style, 32

ngaah choy (pea sprouts), 21–23

ngaah choy chow haah (pea sprouts braised with shrimps), 105

ngaah choy chow jüh yook (pea sprouts braised pork), 149

ngaap (duck), 110

ngow (oxen), 131

ngow baak naam (hundred abdomen of beef), 20, 36, 37

ngung faah yook (five-flowered-pork), 20, 36

ngung faah yook mun sün (salted bamboo braised with pork), 157

ngung heung (spices of five fragrances), 33

ngung lao yü (five willows fish), 97

onions *(choong)*, 23, 24

oysters, dried Chinese *(ho see)*, 29

oyster sauce *(ho yow)*, 32

parsley, Chinese *(yien say)*, 24

pay daahn (ancient eggs), 93

pea sprouts *(ngaah choy)*, 21, 23

peas, snow *(haw laahn dow)*, 24

pigeon *(baak gup)*, 111

pork, five flowered *(ngung faah yook)*, 20, 36

Poultry, 110–129:

  chicken, barbecued *(sieu ghuy)*, 112

    bell pepper braised *(ching jew chow ghuy pien)*, 118

    braised satin *(waaht ghuy)*, 116

    chessmen *(kay jee ghuy)*, 115

    chestnuts *(foong lüt ghuy)*, 121

    curried *(gaah li ghuy)*, 119

    light-shade skewered *(yum yeung ghuy)*, 112

    livers, sweet sour *(tiem shün ghuy gon)*, 120

    mushrooms braised velvet *(maw gwooh chow ghuy pien)*, 116

    paper-wrapped *(jee bow ghuy)*, 113

    pineapple *(baw law ghuy)*, 121

    walnuts *(haap to ghuy)*, 119

    white cut *(baak jaahm ghuy)*, 117

  duck, home-style *(gaah heung ngaap)*, 124

  how to bone, 124

    Peking sauce *(ging jeung ngaap)*, 125

    pineapple *(baw law ngaap)*, 129

    roast *(sieu ngaap)*, 127

    yams braised with *(woo tao ngaap)*, 213

  squab, browned *(jaah baak gup)*, 122

    steamed velvet *(ching jing baak gup)*, 122

  squabs, casserole of mushroom *(maw gwooh mun baak gup)*, 123

Rice and Mien Dishes, 160–168:

  congee, pork *(jüh yook jook)*, 164

    roast duck *(sieu ngaap jook)*, 165

  joong, salty *(haahm joong)*, 198

    sweet *(tiem joong)*, 201

  noodles, broth *(tong mien)*, 168

    Ieh Fooh *(Ieh Fooh mien)*, 167

    how to prepare, 165

    long life *(cheung sao mien)*, 166

  rice, eight-treasure *(baat bo faahn)*, 173

    fried No. 1 *(chow faahn No. 1)*, 163

    fried No. 2 *(chow faahn No. 2)*, 163

    lotus leaf *(haw yeep faahn)*, 216

    white *(baak faahn)*, 162

saang choy yü tong (lettuce and fish soup), 75

saang see jeung (aromatic red beans), 32

sauces, Chinese *(jeung)*, 32, 33

scallion, 23, 24

scallops, dried *(gon yui chee)*, 33

sieu ghuy (barbecued chicken), 112

sieu jüh (roast pig), 134

sieu ngaap (roast duck), 127

sieu ngaap jook (roast duck congee), 165

sieu pi gwut (barbecued spareribs), 138

sook muy daahn faak tong (fresh corn egg flower soup), 79

sou gock (flaky pastry), 56

Soups, 74–86:
  abalone *(bow yü tong)*, 78
  chicken liver *(ghuy gon tong)*, 76
  Chinese cabbage *(baak choy tong)*, 74
  Chinese watercress *(gwaah jee choy tong)*, 77
  fish tripe, clear broth *(ching tong yü to)*, 85
  fresh corn egg flower *(sook muy daahn faah tong)*, 79
  lettuce and fish *(saang choy yü tong)*, 75
  lotus root *(lien ngow tong)*, 79
  melted asparagus *(ghuy yoong low sün)*, 81
  pigeon, broth of *(dun baak gup)*, 81
  pig's feet soya bean *(jüh gerk fooh jook tong)*, 80
  swallow's nest *(ghuy yoong yien waw)*, 85
  velvet chicken broth *wun tun* *(ghuy tong wun tun)*, 69
  watercress *(suy yeung choy tong)*, 76
  winter melon pond *(doong gwaah joong)*, 82
soya bean products *(fooh jook)*, 30, 31
  tiem jock, 30, 31
  bean curd cheese, 32, 33
  bean curd cheese, eastern style, 32
soya sauce *(jeung yow)*, 21, 32
spices, Chinese *(ngung heung)*, 33–35
squash, Chinese (vegetable marrow—*faahn gwaah*), 26
sup gum jaai choy (vegetarian dish), 209
suy yeung choy tong (watercress soup), 76

tiem jook (soya bean), 30, 31
tiem joong (sweet *joong*), 201
tiem shün ghuy gon (sweet-sour chicken livers), 120

tiem shün jüh gerk No. 1 and No. 2 sweet-sour pig's feet No. 1 and No. 2), 139–40
tiem shün pi gwut (sweet-sour spareribs), 138
tiem shün yü (sweet-sour pungent fish), 97
tong (Chinese soups), 74
tong mien (broth noodles), 168
tong yuen (soup globes), 187

Vegetables (with meat), 145–159:
  bamboo, salted braised with pork *(ngung faah yook mun sün)*, 157
  bean curds, oyster sauce *(ho yow dow fooh)*, 155
  bitter melon stuffed with meat *(yeung fooh gwaah)*, 158
  broccoli braised with roast pork *(gaai laan chow chaah sieu)*, 156
  cow peas braised with pork *(dow gock chow jüh yook)*, 157
  chilied mince meat *(laat jew jeung)*, 150
  eggplant braised with pork *(keh chow jüh yook)*, 159
  fried tasty meat mince *(chow yook soong)*, 154
  lima beans braised with pork *(dow chow jüh yook)*, 150
  pea sprouts braised pork *(ngaah choy chow jüh yook)*, 149
  pickled cabbage steamed with pork *(mooi choy jing yook bang)*, 152
  squash braised with beef *(faahn gwaah chow ngow yook)*, 155
  tea melons steamed with pork *(chaah gwaah jing jüh yook)*, 153
  tomato braised with beef *(faahn keh chow ngow yook)*, 151
  turnips braised with beef *(law baak chow ngow yook)*, 153
  vegetarian dish *(sup gum jaai choy)*, 209

225

waaht ghuy (braised satin chicken), 116
water chestnuts *(maah tuy)*, 31, 32
wock, 19, 37
woo tao ngaap (yams braised with duck), 213
woon dow chow daahn (scrambled eggs and peas), 91
wun tun (cloud swallows), 65
wun yee (cloud ears), 27
wuy deep (surrounding dishes), 47

Yang Chow haah kow (Yang Chow shrimp balls), 108
Yang Chow see jee tao (Yang Chow lion's head), 141

yeung (essence of light), 87, 110
yeung (sheep), 132
yeung fooh gwaah (bitter melon stuffed with meat), 158
yeung gwaah (stuffed braised squash), 102
yeung yü (stuffed fish), 98
yien say (Chinese parsley), 24
yü (fish), 96
yü to (fish tripe), 84
yü yeung fooh gwaah (bitter melon stuffed with fish), 103
yuen taai (round ham of pork), 135
yum yeung ghuy (light-shade skewered chicken), 112